Dash Diet Cookbook For Beginners

30-Day Weight Loss Meal Plan, 1800 Days of Delicious Low-Sodium Dash Diet Recipes For Beginners To Lower Blood Pressure. Easy Meal Prep, Ultimate Guide to Health & Wellness

Alanna Elliott

Copyright 2024-All rights reserved.

This document is geared towards providing exact and reliable information regarding the topic and issue covered.

From a Declaration of Principles, accepted and approved equally by a Committee of the American Bar Association and a Committee of Publishers and Associations.

It is not legal to reproduce, duplicate, or transmit any part of this document in either electronic means or printed format. All rights reserved.

The information provided herein is stated to be truthful and consistent in that any liability, in terms of inattention or otherwise, by any usage or abuse of any policies, processes, or directions contained within is the solitary and utter responsibility of the recipient reader. Under no circumstances will any legal responsibility or blame be held against the publisher for any reparation, damages, or monetary loss due to the information herein, either directly or indirectly. Respective authors own all copyrights not held by the publisher.

The information herein is offered for informational purposes solely and is universal as so. The presentation of the information is without a contract or any type of guarantee assurance. The trademarks that are used are without any consent, and the publication of the trademark is without permission or backing by the trademark owner. All trademarks and brands within this book are for clarifying purposes only and are owned by the owners themselves, not affiliated with this document.

Table of Contents

CHAPTER 1 OVERVIEW OF THE DASH DIET.......5
Understanding the DASH Diet................................ 6
How the DASH diet promotes heart health and lowers blood pressure................................ 6
Tips for grocery shopping and meal planning........7
Essential ingredients for DASH-friendly recipes................................ 8

CHAPTER 2 BREAKFAST RECIPES...................... 9
Oatmeal with Fresh Fruit................................ 10
Vegetable Omelette for DASH Diet.....................10
Whole Grain Pancakes with Blueberry Compote..11
Avocado Toast with Poached Egg................. 11
Quinoa Breakfast Bowl................................ 12
Whole Wheat Breakfast Burrito...................... 12
Chia Seed Pudding with Mixed Berries................ 13
Smoked Salmon and Avocado Bagel...................13
Spinach and Feta Egg Muffins........................ 14
Sweet Potato Hash with Turkey Sausage...............14

CHAPTER 3 LUNCH IDEAS.................................15
Turkey and Avocado Wrap................................ 16
Grilled Chicken and Vegetable Skewers............... 16
Mediterranean Eggplant and Zucchini Bake.......... 17
Salmon and Asparagus Foil Packets.................. 17
Chicken and Brown Rice Stir-Fry..................... 18
Quinoa and Black Bean Stuffed Peppers.............. 18
Veggie and Lentil Soup................................19
Vegetable Stir-Fry with Brown Rice................. 19
Hummus and Veggie Sandwich........................ 20
Shrimp and Veggie Skewers............................. 20

CHAPTER 4 DINNER RECIPES........................21
Baked Sweet Potato with Black Bean Salsa............22
Black Bean and Corn Quesadillas.................... 22
Ratatouille with Herbed Couscous....................23

Teriyaki Tofu Stir-Fry................................ 23
Stuffed Portobello Mushrooms.........................24
Baked Cod with Tomato and Olive Relish............... 24
Spaghetti Squash with Marinara Sauce.................25
Turkey Meatballs in Marinara Sauce................... 25
Vegetable and Lentil Curry............................26
Eggplant Parmesan.................................... 26

CHAPTER 5 SOUPS.. 27
Italian Wedding Soup...................................28
Mushroom Soup..28
Chicken and Vegetable Soup......................... 29
Split Pea Soup.. 29
Broccoli Cheddar Soup................................ 30
Butternut Squash Soup................................30
Tomato Basil Soup................................... 31
Spinach and White Bean Soup........................ 31
Moroccan Chickpea Soup...............................32
Vegetable Barley Soup................................ 32

CHAPTER 6 MEAT & POULTRY............................. 33
Baked Garlic Parmesan Chicken....................... 34
Turkey Meatloaf with Tomato Glaze....................34
Mediterranean Stuffed Chicken Breasts............... 35
Herb-Marinated Grilled Steak........................ 35
Balsamic Glazed Pork Chops..........................36
Honey Mustard Glazed Chicken Thighs.................36
Greek Style Grilled Lamb Chops...................... 37
Pesto Turkey Meatballs................................ 37
Orange Glazed Grilled Chicken........................38
Italian Herb Crusted Pork Tenderloin.................38

CHAPTER 7 FISH & SEAFOOD............................. 39
Spicy Sriracha Tuna Cakes............................40
Baked Dijon Tilapia...................................40
Shrimp Stir-Fry with Vegetables...................... 41

Teriyaki Glazed Mahi Mahi 41
Mediterranean Baked Halibut 42
Garlic Parmesan Crusted Salmon 42
Lemon Garlic Butter Scallops 43
Herb Crusted Baked Snapper 43
Garlic Butter Lemon Shrimp Pasta 44
Baked Lemon Herb Trout 44

CHAPTER 8 SALADS 45
Tuna Nicoise Salad 46
Spinach and Strawberry Salad 46
Kale and Apple Salad with Lemon Vinaigrette 47
Beet and Goat Cheese Salad 47
Cobb Salad with Grilled Chicken 48
Asian Cucumber Salad 48
Waldorf Salad with Yogurt Dressing 49
Arugula and Pear Salad with Walnuts 49
Watermelon and Feta Salad with Mint 50
Orange and Fennel Salad 50

CHAPTER 9 SNACKS AND APPETIZERS 51
Greek Yogurt Dip with Vegetables 52
Hummus and Whole Wheat Pita Chips 52
Cottage Cheese with Pineapple Chunks 53
Whole Grain Crackers with Tzatziki 53
Deviled Eggs with Avocado 54
Spicy Edamame 54
Smoked Salmon Cucumber Bites 55
Baked Sweet Potato Fries 55
Antipasto Skewers with Olives and Cherry Tomatoes 56
Almond and Date Energy Balls 56

CHAPTER 10 DESSERTS AND TREATS 57
Avocado Chocolate Mousse 58
Banana Oatmeal Cookies 58
Mango Coconut Popsicles 59
Lemon Blueberry Muffins with Whole Wheat Flour 59
Almond Flour Chocolate Chip Cookies 60

Apple Cinnamon Quinoa Breakfast Bars 60
Strawberry Banana Nice Cream 61
Pumpkin Spice Energy Balls 61
Orange Cranberry Oatmeal Cookies 62
Coconut Flour Pancakes with Fresh Fruit 62

CHAPTER 11 BEVERAGES & TEAS 63
Green Smoothie with Spinach and Banana 64
Lemon Ginger Tea 64
Berry Blast Smoothie 65
Golden Turmeric Latte 65
Strawberry Basil Lemonade 66
Hibiscus Green Tea 66
Carrot Orange Ginger Juice 67
Cranberry Pomegranate Sparkler 67
Ginger Turmeric Tea 68
Chamomile Lavender Tea 68

CHAPTER 12 BONUSES AND USEFUL MATERIALS 69
30-day Meal Plan 70
Shopping Lists 73
Shopping List for 1-7 day Meal Plan 73
Shopping List for 8-14 day Meal Plan 74
Shopping List for 15-21 day Meal Plan 75
Shopping List for 22-30 day Meal Plan 76
Measurement Conversion Chart 77
Blood Pressure Monitoring List 78

UNDERSTANDING THE DASH DIET

Welcome to the "DASH Diet Cookbook for Beginners," your guide to embracing a healthier and more vibrant lifestyle through the principles of the DASH (Dietary Approaches to Stop Hypertension) diet. In the journey towards overall well-being, a balanced and nutritious diet plays a pivotal role, and the DASH diet stands out as a proven approach to achieving not just a healthy heart but also a healthier you.

The DASH diet is more than just a set of guidelines; it's a way of life that emphasizes whole foods, nutrient-rich ingredients, and mindful eating habits. Originally developed to help individuals lower blood pressure, the DASH diet has evolved into a comprehensive approach to promoting heart health, managing weight, and preventing chronic diseases.

The DASH diet is a dietary plan specifically designed to help prevent and manage hypertension, commonly known as high blood pressure. Developed by the National Heart, Lung, and Blood Institute (NHLBI), the DASH diet emphasizes a balanced and heart-healthy approach to eating. It has gained recognition not only for its effectiveness in reducing blood pressure but also for its overall benefits in promoting cardiovascular health.

Key Principles:

- **Focus on Whole Foods:** The DASH diet encourages the consumption of whole, nutrient-dense foods. This includes fruits, vegetables, whole grains, lean proteins, and low-fat dairy products.
- **Reduced Sodium Intake:** A significant aspect of the DASH diet is the limitation of sodium (salt) intake. Lowering sodium levels contributes to the prevention and management of high blood pressure.
- **Moderation in Fats and Sweets:** While not overly restrictive, the DASH diet recommends moderation in the consumption of fats, especially saturated fats and sweets.
- **Rich in Potassium, Calcium, and Magnesium:** The diet emphasizes foods high in potassium, calcium, and magnesium, which are minerals linked to blood pressure regulation. These nutrients are found abundantly in fruits, vegetables, and low-fat dairy products.
- **Balanced Macronutrients:** The DASH diet seeks a balanced distribution of macronutrients, including carbohydrates, proteins, and fats.

Health Benefits:

- **Blood Pressure Management:** The primary goal of the DASH diet is to prevent and control hypertension. Studies have shown that adhering to the DASH dietary pattern can lead to significant reductions in blood pressure.
- **Heart Health:** Beyond blood pressure, the DASH diet is associated with improved cardiovascular health. It helps lower cholesterol levels and reduce the risk of heart disease.
- **Weight Management:** The emphasis on whole, nutrient-dense foods and portion control in the DASH diet can contribute to weight management and a healthier body mass index (BMI).

One of the strengths of the DASH diet is its adaptability. It can be customized to meet individual preferences, cultural dietary patterns, and specific health goals. Whether you're a vegetarian, omnivore, or have dietary restrictions, the DASH diet can be tailored to suit your needs.

In summary, the DASH diet is a flexible and evidence-based approach to eating that promotes heart health, lowers blood pressure, and supports overall well-being through a balanced and varied diet.

HOW THE DASH DIET PROMOTES HEART HEALTH AND LOWERS BLOOD PRESSURE

The DASH diet is specifically designed to promote heart health and lower blood pressure. It achieves these goals through several key mechanisms:

Reduced Sodium Intake: One of the primary contributors to high blood pressure is excessive sodium intake. The DASH diet recommends reducing sodium levels, which helps regulate fluid balance and decreases the strain on the cardiovascular system.

High Potassium Intake: The DASH diet is rich in potassium, a mineral that counteracts the effects of sodium. Potassium helps relax blood vessel walls, reducing blood pressure. Foods high in potassium, such as fruits, vegetables, and low-fat dairy, are prominent in the DASH diet.

Balanced Macronutrients: The DASH diet emphasizes a balanced distribution of macronutrients, including carbohydrates, proteins, and fats. This balance supports overall cardiovascular health by providing necessary nutrients without overloading the body with unhealthy fats or excessive calories.

Increased Magnesium and Calcium Intake: Magnesium and calcium are minerals that play a role in blood pressure regulation. The DASH diet includes foods rich in these minerals, such as nuts, seeds, dairy products, and leafy green vegetables.

Promotion of Healthy Fats: The diet encourages the consumption of healthy fats, such as those found in olive oil, avocados, and nuts. These fats have been associated with a reduced risk of heart disease and contribute to overall cardiovascular health.

Emphasis on Whole Foods: Whole, nutrient-dense foods, such as fruits, vegetables, whole grains, and lean proteins, are staples of the DASH diet. These foods provide essential vitamins, minerals, and antioxidants that support heart health.

Fiber-Rich Diet: The DASH diet is high in dietary fiber, which has multiple cardiovascular benefits. Fiber helps lower cholesterol levels, improve blood vessel function, and stabilize blood sugar levels.

Weight Management: By promoting a balanced diet and portion control, the DASH diet helps individuals maintain a healthy weight. Excess weight is a risk factor for high blood pressure and heart disease.

Antioxidant Protection: Many foods included in the DASH diet are rich in antioxidants, which help protect the heart and blood vessels from oxidative stress. This includes fruits, vegetables, and whole grains.

Overall Heart-Healthy Lifestyle: The DASH diet is often accompanied by recommendations for a heart-healthy lifestyle, including regular physical activity, limited alcohol intake, and avoidance of smoking. These lifestyle factors contribute to a comprehensive approach to cardiovascular well-being.

TIPS FOR GROCERY SHOPPING AND MEAL PLANNING

Grocery Shopping Tips:

Make a List: Plan your meals for the week and create a shopping list. Stick to the list to avoid impulsive purchases.

Shop the Perimeter: Focus on the perimeter of the grocery store where fresh produce, lean proteins, and dairy products are typically located. This helps you choose whole, minimally processed foods.

Choose Fresh Produce: Select a variety of colorful fruits and vegetables. These are rich in vitamins, minerals, and antioxidants, and they are fundamental to the DASH diet.

Opt for Whole Grains: Choose whole grains like brown rice, quinoa, whole wheat pasta, and oats. These provide fiber and essential nutrients recommended by the DASH diet.

Select Lean Proteins: Choose lean protein sources such as skinless poultry, fish, beans, lentils, and tofu. Limit red meat and opt for lean cuts.

Go for Low-Fat Dairy: Choose low-fat or fat-free dairy products. These provide essential nutrients like calcium and are in line with the DASH diet recommendations.

Read Labels: Check food labels for sodium content. Choose products with lower sodium levels and be mindful of hidden sources of added salt.

Stock Up on Healthy Fats: Include sources of healthy fats like olive oil, avocados, nuts, and seeds. These fats are part of the DASH diet's emphasis on heart-healthy choices.

Limit Processed Foods: Minimize the purchase of processed and pre-packaged foods, which often contain high levels of sodium, added sugars, and unhealthy fats.

Buy in Bulk: Consider buying non-perishable items in bulk to save money. This can include whole grains, beans, and nuts.

Meal Planning Tips:

Plan Balanced Meals: Ensure each meal includes a balance of fruits, vegetables, lean proteins, whole grains, and healthy fats.

Cook in Batches: Prepare larger quantities of meals and freeze portions for later use. This helps with time management and ensures you have healthy options readily available.

Use Leftovers Creatively: Repurpose leftovers into new meals to avoid food waste. For example, grilled chicken can be used in salads, wraps, or stir-fries.

Include a Variety of Foods: Rotate through different fruits, vegetables, proteins, and whole grains to ensure

a diverse and nutrient-rich diet.

Mindful Portion Control: Be conscious of portion sizes to avoid overeating. The DASH diet emphasizes balanced meals with appropriate portion sizes.

Prep Ingredients in Advance: Wash, chop, and portion out ingredients ahead of time. This makes cooking during the week more efficient.

Experiment with DASH-Friendly Recipes: Explore new recipes that align with the DASH diet. This adds variety to your meals and keeps your diet interesting.

Consider Seasonal Produce: Incorporate seasonal fruits and vegetables into your meal plans. They are often more affordable and fresher.

Plan for Snacks: Have healthy snacks, such as fresh fruit, vegetables with hummus, or Greek yogurt, readily available to prevent unhealthy snacking.

Stay Hydrated: Remember to include water as a beverage of choice. Staying hydrated is an important aspect of the DASH diet.

By combining these grocery shopping and meal planning tips, you can establish a routine that aligns with the DASH diet principles and supports your overall health and well-being.

ESSENTIAL INGREDIENTS FOR DASH-FRIENDLY RECIPES

Creating DASH-friendly recipes involves incorporating nutrient-dense, heart-healthy ingredients that align with the principles of the Dietary Approaches to Stop Hypertension (DASH) diet. Here's a list of essential ingredients for DASH-friendly recipes:

- **Fruits:** berries (blueberries, strawberries, raspberries), apples, bananas, oranges, kiwi, pineapple, mango.
- **Vegetables:** leafy greens (spinach, kale, swiss chard), broccoli, bell peppers (various colors), tomatoes, carrots, cauliflower, zucchini.
- **Whole Grains:** brown rice, quinoa, barley, whole wheat pasta, oats, bulgur, farro.
- **Lean Proteins:** skinless poultry (chicken, turkey), fish (salmon, trout, tuna), lean cuts of beef or pork, beans (black beans, kidney beans, chickpeas), lentils, tofu, eggs.
- **Dairy or Dairy Alternatives:** low-fat or fat-free yogurt, skim milk, low-fat cheese, plant-based milk alternatives (almond milk, soy milk).
- **Healthy Fats:** olive oil, avocados, nuts (almonds, walnuts, pistachios), seeds (flaxseeds, chia seeds, sunflower seeds).
- **Herbs and Spices:** garlic, ginger, basil, oregano, thyme, cumin, turmeric.
- **Low-Sodium Condiments:** herbs and vinegar for salad dressings, low-sodium soy sauce, dijon mustard, salsa (low-sodium), tomato paste.
- **High-Fiber Foods:** beans and legumes, whole grains, fruits (especially with skins), vegetables.
- **Fresh Herbs for Flavor:** parsley, cilantro, mint, rosemary, dill.
- **Whole Wheat Flour:** use for baking to increase the fiber content.
- **Sweeteners in Moderation:** honey, maple syrup, agave nectar.
- **Plant-Based Proteins:** incorporate more plant-based protein sources like legumes, tofu, and tempeh.
- **Low-Sodium Canned Goods:** tomatoes (diced or crushed), beans (rinsed to reduce sodium content).
- **Nuts and Seeds:** almonds, walnuts, chia seeds, flaxseeds.
- **Non-Starchy Vegetables:** asparagus, brussels sprouts, cabbage, cucumber.
- **Beverages:** water, herbal teas, unsweetened plant-based milk.
- **Fish Oil or Omega-3 Supplements:** for those who may have difficulty getting enough omega-3 fatty acids through food alone.

By incorporating these essential ingredients into your DASH-friendly recipes, you can create flavorful and nutritious meals that contribute to heart health and overall well-being. Adjust portion sizes and be mindful of overall sodium intake for optimal results.

Integrating these principles into your daily eating habits can help you experience the benefits of the DASH diet, including lower blood pressure, reduced risk of heart disease, and overall improved heart health. It's important to note that consultation with a healthcare professional or registered dietitian is recommended before making significant dietary changes, especially for individuals with existing health conditions.

OATMEAL WITH FRESH FRUIT

4 servings | Prep time: 5 minutes | Cook time: 10 minutes

Ingredients:
- 1 cup old-fashioned oats
- 2 cups water
- 1 cup low-fat milk
- 1 teaspoon vanilla extract
- 1/4 teaspoon cinnamon
- Pinch of salt
- 1 cup mixed fresh berries (strawberries, blueberries, raspberries)
- 1 medium banana, sliced
- 1 tablespoon honey or maple syrup (optional)
- Chopped nuts (almonds, walnuts) for garnish (optional)

Directions:
1. In a medium saucepan, bring the water and milk to a gentle boil over medium heat.
2. Stir in the oats, vanilla extract, cinnamon, and a pinch of salt. Reduce the heat to low and simmer, stirring occasionally, for about 8-10 minutes or until the oats are tender and have absorbed most of the liquid.
3. Remove the saucepan from the heat and let it stand for a couple of minutes to thicken.
4. Divide the oatmeal among serving bowls.
5. Top each bowl with a generous portion of mixed fresh berries and banana slices.
6. Drizzle with honey or maple syrup if desired.
7. Garnish with chopped nuts for added flavor.
8. Serve warm and enjoy!

Nutritional Information per serving:
Cal: 220 | Fat: 3g | Chol: 2mg | Sodium: 40mg | Carbs: 45g | Fiber: 7g | Sugars: 15g | Protein: 7g

VEGETABLE OMELETTE FOR DASH DIET

2 servings | Prep time: 10 minutes | Cook time: 10 minutes

Ingredients:
- 4 large eggs
- 1/4 cup low-fat milk
- Salt and black pepper, to taste
- 1 tablespoon olive oil
- 1/2 cup diced bell peppers (mixed colors)
- 1/2 cup diced tomatoes
- 1/2 cup chopped spinach leaves
- 1/4 cup diced red onions
- 1/4 cup reduced-fat feta cheese, crumbled
- Fresh herbs (such as parsley or chives) for garnish

Directions:
1. Whisk together eggs, low-fat milk, salt, and black pepper until well combined.
2. Heat olive oil in a non-stick skillet over medium heat.
3. Add bell peppers, tomatoes, spinach, and red onions to the skillet. Sauté for 3-4 minutes until the vegetables are slightly tender.
4. Pour the egg mixture evenly over the sautéed vegetables.
5. Allow the edges to set, then gently lift them with a spatula to let the uncooked eggs flow underneath.
6. Once the omelette is mostly set but still slightly runny on top, sprinkle crumbled feta cheese over one half of the omelette.
7. Carefully fold the other half of the omelette over the cheese side, creating a half-moon shape.
8. Continue cooking for an additional 1-2 minutes until the cheese is melted.
9. Slide the omelette onto a plate, garnish with fresh herbs.

Nutritional Information per serving:
Cal: 250 | Fat: 17g | Chol: 370mg | Sodium: 380mg | Carbs: 9g | Fiber: 2g | Sugars: 5g | Protein: 16g

WHOLE GRAIN PANCAKES WITH BLUEBERRY COMPOTE

4 servings | Prep time: 15 minutes | Cook time: 15 minutes

Ingredients:
- 1 cup whole wheat flour
- 1 tablespoon sugar
- 1 teaspoon baking powder
- 1/2 teaspoon baking soda
- 1 cup low-fat buttermilk
- 1 large egg
- 2 tablespoons unsalted butter, melted
- 1 teaspoon vanilla extract
- Blueberry Compote (fresh or frozen blueberries, a touch of honey)

Directions:
1. In a bowl, whisk together whole wheat flour, sugar, baking powder, and baking soda.
2. In a separate bowl, mix buttermilk, egg, melted butter, and vanilla extract.
3. Combine the wet and dry ingredients, stirring until just combined.
4. Heat a griddle or skillet over medium heat and ladle the pancake batter onto the surface.
5. Cook until bubbles form on the surface, then flip and cook until golden brown on both sides.
6. Serve with a generous spoonful of blueberry compote.

Nutritional Information per serving:
Cal: 250 | Fat: 7g | Chol: 50mg | Sodium: 300mg | Carbs: 40g | Fiber: 5g | Sugars: 10g | Protein: 8g

AVOCADO TOAST WITH POACHED EGG

2 servings | Prep time: 10 minutes | Cook time: 5 minutes

Ingredients:
- 2 slices whole grain bread, toasted
- 1 ripe avocado, mashed
- Salt and black pepper, to taste
- 2 large eggs, poached
- Optional toppings: red pepper flakes, cherry tomatoes, or fresh herbs

Directions:
1. Spread mashed avocado evenly on toasted whole grain bread slices.
2. Season with salt and black pepper.
3. Top each slice with a poached egg.
4. Garnish with red pepper flakes, cherry tomatoes, or fresh herbs if desired.

Nutritional Information per serving:
Cal: 300 | Fat: 18g | Chol: 185mg | Sodium: 250mg | Carbs: 26g | Fiber: 10g | Sugars: 2g | Protein: 12g

QUINOA BREAKFAST BOWL

2 servings | Prep time: 15 minutes | Cook time: 15 minutes

Ingredients:
- 1 cup cooked quinoa
- 1 cup low-fat Greek yogurt
- 1 cup mixed berries (strawberries, blueberries, raspberries)
- 1 tablespoon honey
- 2 tablespoons chopped nuts (almonds, walnuts)

Directions:
1. Divide cooked quinoa between two bowls.
2. Top with Greek yogurt and mixed berries.
3. Drizzle with honey and sprinkle chopped nuts over the top.

Nutritional Information per serving:
Cal: 320 | Fat: 10g | Chol: 10mg | Sodium: 60mg | Carbs: 50g | Fiber: 7g | Sugars: 20g | Protein: 15g

WHOLE WHEAT BREAKFAST BURRITO

2 servings | Prep time: 10 minutes | Cook time: 10 minutes

Ingredients:
- 4 large eggs, scrambled
- 1 cup black beans, cooked
- 1 cup diced tomatoes
- 1/2 cup diced red onions
- 1/2 cup shredded reduced-fat cheese
- 2 whole wheat tortillas
- Salsa and fresh cilantro for garnish

Directions:
1. In a skillet, scramble eggs until just cooked.
2. Warm tortillas in the skillet or microwave.
3. Assemble burritos by layering eggs, black beans, tomatoes, red onions, and cheese on each tortilla.
4. Roll up the burritos and garnish with salsa and fresh cilantro.

Nutritional Information per serving:
Cal: 380 | Fat: 14g | Chol: 340mg | Sodium: 480mg | Carbs: 40g | Fiber: 10g | Sugars: 5g | Protein: 25g

CHIA SEED PUDDING WITH MIXED BERRIES

SMOKED SALMON AND AVOCADO BAGEL

2 servings | Prep time: 5 minutes | Chill time: 4 hours or overnight

2 servings | Prep time: 10 minutes

Ingredients:
- 1/4 cup chia seeds
- 1 cup unsweetened almond milk
- 1 teaspoon vanilla extract
- 1 cup mixed berries (strawberries, blueberries, raspberries)
- Optional: drizzle of honey or maple syrup

Ingredients:
- 2 whole grain bagels, toasted
- 1 ripe avocado, sliced
- 4 ounces smoked salmon
- 1 tablespoon capers
- Fresh dill for garnish

Directions:
1. In a bowl, mix chia seeds, almond milk, and vanilla extract.
2. Stir well and refrigerate for at least 4 hours or overnight.
3. Before serving, stir the pudding to ensure a smooth consistency.
4. Divide the chia seed pudding into two bowls and top with mixed berries.
5. Drizzle with honey or maple syrup if desired.

Directions:
1. Toast whole grain bagels until golden brown.
2. Spread sliced avocado on each half of the bagels.
3. Top with smoked salmon and sprinkle with capers.
4. Garnish with fresh dill.

Nutritional Information per serving:
Cal: 320 | Fat: 15g | Chol: 15mg | Sodium: 500mg | Carbs: 35g | Fiber: 9g | Sugars: 2g | Protein: 20g

Nutritional Information per serving:
Cal: 200 | Fat: 10g | Chol: 0mg | Sodium: 70mg | Carbs: 25g | Fiber: 12g | Sugars: 8g | Protein: 5g

SPINACH AND FETA EGG MUFFINS

4 servings | Prep time: 10 minutes | Cook time: 20 minutes

Ingredients:
- 6 large eggs
- 1 cup chopped spinach
- 1/2 cup crumbled reduced-fat feta cheese
- 1/4 cup diced red bell pepper
- Salt and black pepper, to taste
- Cooking spray

Directions:
1. Preheat the oven to 350°F (175°C). Grease a muffin tin with cooking spray.
2. In a bowl, whisk together eggs, spinach, feta cheese, red bell pepper, salt, and black pepper.
3. Pour the egg mixture evenly into the muffin tin.
4. Bake for about 20 minutes or until the eggs are set.
5. Allow the egg muffins to cool slightly before removing them from the tin.

Nutritional Information per serving:
Cal: 150 | Fat: 10g | Chol: 215mg | Sodium: 280mg | Carbs: 3g | Fiber: 1g | Sugars: 2g | Protein: 12g

SWEET POTATO HASH WITH TURKEY SAUSAGE

4 servings | Prep time: 15 minutes | Cook time: 20 minutes

Ingredients:
- 2 medium sweet potatoes, peeled and diced
- 1/2 pound lean turkey sausage, crumbled
- 1 red bell pepper, diced
- 1 yellow onion, diced
- 2 cloves garlic, minced
- 1 teaspoon smoked paprika
- Salt and black pepper, to taste
- Olive oil for cooking
- Fresh parsley for garnish

Directions:
1. In a large skillet, heat olive oil over medium heat.
2. Add sweet potatoes and cook until they begin to soften.
3. Add crumbled turkey sausage, bell pepper, onion, and garlic to the skillet.
4. Season with smoked paprika, salt, and black pepper.
5. Cook until sweet potatoes are tender and sausage is fully cooked.
6. Garnish with fresh parsley before serving.

Nutritional Information per serving:
Cal: 280 | Fat: 10g | Chol: 45mg | Sodium: 480mg | Carbs: 30g | Fiber: 5g | Sugars: 7g | Protein: 18g

Chapter 3
LUNCH IDEAS

TURKEY AND AVOCADO WRAP

Yield: 2 servings | Prep time: 10 minutes | Cook time: 0 minutes

Ingredients:

- 4 whole wheat tortillas
- 8 slices of deli turkey breast
- 1 ripe avocado, sliced
- 1 cup mixed greens
- 1/2 cup shredded carrots
- 1/4 cup diced tomatoes
- 1/4 cup diced red onions
- 2 tablespoons plain Greek yogurt
- 1 tablespoon Dijon mustard
- Salt and pepper to taste

Directions:

1. Lay out the whole wheat tortillas on a clean surface.
2. In a small bowl, mix together Greek yogurt and Dijon mustard. Spread the mixture evenly onto each tortilla.
3. Layer two slices of turkey breast onto each tortilla.
4. Top with avocado slices, mixed greens, shredded carrots, diced tomatoes, and diced red onions.
5. Season with salt and pepper to taste.
6. Roll up the tortillas tightly, folding in the sides as you go.
7. Slice the wraps in half and serve immediately.

Nutritional Information per serving:

Cal: 370 | Fat: 17g | Chol: 30mg | Sodium: 650mg | Carbs: 38g | Fiber: 9g | Sugars: 5g | Protein: 20g

GRILLED CHICKEN AND VEGETABLE SKEWERS

Yield: 2 servings | Prep time: 20 minutes | Cook time: 10 minutes

Ingredients:

- 2 boneless, skinless chicken breasts, cut into chunks
- 1 zucchini, sliced
- 1 yellow bell pepper, cut into chunks
- 1 red onion, cut into chunks
- 8 cherry tomatoes
- 2 tablespoons olive oil
- 1 teaspoon dried oregano
- Salt and pepper to taste

Directions:

1. Preheat grill to medium-high heat.
2. Thread chicken chunks, zucchini slices, bell pepper chunks, red onion chunks, and cherry tomatoes onto skewers.
3. In a small bowl, mix together olive oil, dried oregano, salt, and pepper. Brush the mixture onto the skewers.
4. Grill the skewers for 8-10 minutes, turning occasionally, until chicken is cooked through and vegetables are tender.
5. Serve the grilled chicken and vegetable skewers immediately.

Nutritional Information per serving:

Cal: 230 | Fat: 10g | Chol: 60mg | Sodium: 70mg | Carbs: 8g | Fiber: 2g | Sugars: 4g | Protein: 25g

MEDITERRANEAN EGGPLANT AND ZUCCHINI BAKE

Yield: 4 servings | Prep time: 15 minutes | Cook time: 25 minutes

Ingredients:
- 1 eggplant, sliced
- 2 zucchinis, sliced
- 1 bell pepper, sliced
- 1 red onion, sliced
- 2 cloves garlic, minced
- 2 tablespoons olive oil
- 1 teaspoon dried oregano
- 1/2 teaspoon dried thyme
- Salt and pepper to taste
- 1/4 cup crumbled feta cheese
- Fresh parsley for garnish

Directions:
1. Preheat oven to 400°F (200°C). Grease a baking dish with olive oil.
2. Arrange eggplant slices, zucchini slices, bell pepper slices, and red onion slices in the baking dish.
3. Drizzle olive oil over the vegetables. Sprinkle minced garlic, dried oregano, dried thyme, salt, and pepper.
4. Toss the vegetables until evenly coated with the seasonings.
5. Bake for 20-25 minutes until vegetables are tender and lightly browned.
6. Remove from the oven and sprinkle crumbled feta cheese and fresh parsley over the top.
7. Serve the Mediterranean eggplant and zucchini bake hot or at room temperature.

Nutritional Information per serving:
Cal: 180 | Fat: 10g | Chol: 0mg | Sodium: 20mg | Carbs: 22g | Fiber: 8g | Sugars: 12g | Protein: 4g

SALMON AND ASPARAGUS FOIL PACKETS

Yield: 2 servings | Prep time: 10 minutes | Cook time: 20 minutes

Ingredients:
- 2 salmon fillets
- 1 bunch asparagus, trimmed
- 2 tablespoons olive oil
- 2 cloves garlic, minced
- 1 lemon, sliced
- Salt and pepper to taste
- Fresh dill for garnish

Directions:
1. Preheat oven to 400°F (200°C).
2. Place each salmon fillet in the center of a large piece of foil.
3. Arrange asparagus around the salmon fillets.
4. Drizzle olive oil over the salmon and asparagus. Sprinkle minced garlic, salt, and pepper.
5. Place lemon slices on top of the salmon.
6. Fold the foil over the salmon and asparagus to create packets, sealing tightly.
7. Bake for 15-20 minutes until salmon is cooked through and asparagus is tender.
8. Carefully open the foil packets and transfer the salmon and asparagus to plates.
9. Garnish with fresh dill and serve immediately.

Nutritional Information per serving:
Cal: 350 | Fat: 21g | Chol: 80mg | Sodium: 80mg | Carbs: 7g | Fiber: 3g | Sugars: 2g | Protein: 34g

CHICKEN AND BROWN RICE STIR-FRY

Yield: 4 servings | Prep time: 15 minutes | Cook time: 20 minutes

Ingredients:
- 2 boneless, skinless chicken breasts, cut into strips
- 2 cups cooked brown rice
- 1 cup broccoli florets
- 1 red bell pepper, sliced
- 1 carrot, sliced
- 1/2 cup snap peas
- 2 cloves garlic, minced
- 2 tablespoons low-sodium soy sauce
- 1 tablespoon hoisin sauce
- 1 tablespoon olive oil
- 1 teaspoon sesame oil
- Sesame seeds for garnish

Directions:
1. Heat olive oil in a large skillet or wok over medium-high heat.
2. Add chicken strips and cook until browned and cooked through.
3. Remove chicken from the skillet and set aside.
4. In the same skillet, add minced garlic and sauté for 1 minute.
5. Add broccoli florets, red bell pepper slices, carrot slices, and snap peas to the skillet. Cook until vegetables are tender-crisp.
6. Return cooked chicken to the skillet.
7. Stir in cooked brown rice, low-sodium soy sauce, hoisin sauce, and sesame oil. Cook for an additional 2-3 minutes until heated through.
8. Garnish with sesame seeds and serve the chicken and brown rice stir-fry immediately.

Nutritional Information per serving:
Cal: 320 | Fat: 8g | Chol: 60mg | Sodium: 380mg | Carbs: 36g | Fiber: 4g | Sugars: 3g | Protein: 26g

QUINOA AND BLACK BEAN STUFFED PEPPERS

Yield: 4 servings | Prep time: 15 minutes | Cook time: 30 minutes

Ingredients:
- 4 large bell peppers
- 1 cup cooked quinoa
- 1 cup cooked black beans
- 1 cup diced tomatoes
- 1/2 cup corn kernels
- 1/4 cup diced red onion
- 1/4 cup chopped fresh cilantro
- 1 teaspoon ground cumin
- 1 teaspoon chili powder
- Salt and pepper to taste
- 1/2 cup shredded reduced-fat cheese (optional)

Directions:
1. Preheat oven to 375°F (190°C). Grease a baking dish with olive oil.
2. Slice the tops off the bell peppers and remove the seeds and membranes.
3. In a large bowl, combine cooked quinoa, cooked black beans, diced tomatoes, corn kernels, diced red onion, chopped fresh cilantro, ground cumin, chili powder, salt, and pepper.
4. Stuff each bell pepper with the quinoa and black bean mixture.
5. Place the stuffed peppers in the prepared baking dish.
6. If desired, sprinkle shredded reduced-fat cheese over the top of each stuffed pepper.
7. Cover the baking dish with foil and bake for 25-30 minutes until peppers are tender.
8. Remove foil and bake for an additional 5 minutes until cheese is melted and bubbly.
9. Serve hot.

Nutritional Information per serving:
Cal: 280 | Fat: 4g | Chol: 0mg | Sodium: 240mg | Carbs: 52g | Fiber: 11g | Sugars: 6g | Protein: 13g

VEGGIE AND LENTIL SOUP

Yield: 6 servings | Prep time: 15 minutes | Cook time: 30 minutes

Ingredients:
- 1 tablespoon olive oil
- 1 onion, diced
- 2 carrots, diced
- 2 celery stalks, diced
- 2 cloves garlic, minced
- 1 teaspoon dried thyme
- 1 teaspoon dried oregano
- 1/2 teaspoon ground cumin
- 6 cups vegetable broth
- 1 cup dry green lentils
- 2 cups chopped kale
- Salt and pepper to taste
- Fresh parsley for garnish

Directions:
1. Heat olive oil in a large pot over medium heat.
2. Add diced onion, carrots, and celery. Cook until vegetables are softened, about 5-7 minutes.
3. Add minced garlic, dried thyme, dried oregano, and ground cumin. Cook for an additional 1 minute until fragrant.
4. Pour in vegetable broth and add dry green lentils. Bring to a boil.
5. Reduce heat to low, cover, and simmer for 20-25 minutes until lentils are tender.
6. Stir in chopped kale and cook for an additional 5 minutes until kale is wilted.
7. Season with salt and pepper to taste.
8. Ladle the veggie and lentil soup into bowls, garnish with fresh parsley, and serve hot.

Nutritional Information per serving:
Cal: 210 | Fat: 3g | Chol: 0mg | Sodium: 780mg | Carbs: 34g | Fiber: 12g | Sugars: 5g | Protein: 13g

VEGETABLE STIR-FRY WITH BROWN RICE

Yield: 4 servings | Prep time: 10 minutes | Cook time: 15 minutes

Ingredients:
- 2 cups cooked brown rice
- 1 tablespoon olive oil
- 1 onion, sliced
- 2 bell peppers, sliced
- 2 cups broccoli florets
- 1 cup snap peas
- 2 cloves garlic, minced
- 2 tablespoons low-sodium soy sauce
- 1 tablespoon hoisin sauce
- 1 teaspoon sesame oil
- Sesame seeds for garnish

Directions:
1. Heat olive oil in a large skillet or wok over medium-high heat.
2. Add sliced onion and cook until softened, about 3-4 minutes.
3. Add sliced bell peppers, broccoli florets, snap peas, and minced garlic to the skillet. Cook until vegetables are tender-crisp.
4. Stir in cooked brown rice, low-sodium soy sauce, hoisin sauce, and sesame oil. Cook for an additional 2-3 minutes until heated through.
5. Garnish with sesame seeds and serve the vegetable stir-fry with brown rice immediately.

Nutritional Information per serving:
Cal: 280 | Fat: 6g | Chol: 0mg | Sodium: 580mg | Carbs: 50g | Fiber: 8g | Sugars: 7g | Protein: 9g

HUMMUS AND VEGGIE SANDWICH

Yield: 2 servings | Prep time: 10 minutes | Cook time: 0 minutes

Ingredients:
- 4 slices whole grain bread
- 1/2 cup hummus
- 1 cup mixed salad greens
- 1/2 cup shredded carrots
- 1/2 cup sliced cucumbers
- 1/4 cup sliced red bell peppers
- Salt and pepper to taste

Directions:
1. Spread hummus evenly onto each slice of whole grain bread.
2. Layer mixed salad greens, shredded carrots, sliced cucumbers, and sliced red bell peppers on two slices of bread.
3. Season with salt and pepper to taste.
4. Top with the remaining two slices of bread to form sandwiches.
5. Slice the sandwiches in half and serve immediately.

Nutritional Information per serving:
Cal: 320 | Fat: 12g | Chol: 0mg | Sodium: 650mg | Carbs: 45g | Fiber: 10g | Sugars: 5g | Protein: 12g

SHRIMP AND VEGGIE SKEWERS

Yield: 4 servings | Prep time: 20 minutes | Cook time: 10 minutes

Ingredients:
- 1 pound large shrimp, peeled and deveined
- 1 zucchini, sliced
- 1 yellow bell pepper, cut into chunks
- 1 red onion, cut into chunks
- 8 cherry tomatoes
- 2 tablespoons olive oil
- 1 teaspoon dried oregano
- Salt and pepper to taste
- Lemon wedges for serving

Directions:
1. Preheat grill to medium-high heat.
2. Thread shrimp, zucchini slices, bell pepper chunks, red onion chunks, and cherry tomatoes onto skewers.
3. In a small bowl, mix together olive oil, dried oregano, salt, and pepper. Brush the mixture onto the skewers.
4. Grill the skewers for 4-5 minutes on each side until shrimp are pink and opaque.
5. Serve the shrimp and veggie skewers immediately with lemon wedges.

Nutritional Information per serving:
Cal: 190 | Fat: 8g | Chol: 170mg | Sodium: 400mg | Carbs: 10g | Fiber: 2g | Sugars: 4g | Protein: 18g

BAKED SWEET POTATO WITH BLACK BEAN SALSA

Yield: 4 servings | Prep time: 10 minutes | Cook time: 45 minutes

Ingredients:
- 4 medium sweet potatoes
- 1 can (15 ounces) black beans, rinsed and drained
- 1 cup diced tomatoes
- 1/2 cup diced red onion
- 1/4 cup chopped fresh cilantro
- 1 jalapeno pepper, seeded and minced
- 2 tablespoons lime juice
- 1 teaspoon ground cumin
- Salt and pepper to taste
- Optional toppings: avocado slices, Greek yogurt, lime wedges

Directions:
1. Preheat the oven to 400°F (200°C).
2. Scrub the sweet potatoes and pierce each potato several times with a fork.
3. Place the sweet potatoes on a baking sheet and bake for 45-60 minutes, or until tender.
4. In a large bowl, combine black beans, diced tomatoes, diced red onion, chopped cilantro, minced jalapeno pepper, lime juice, ground cumin, salt, and pepper. Mix well to combine.
5. Once the sweet potatoes are cooked, slice each potato lengthwise and fluff the flesh with a fork.
6. Top each sweet potato with the black bean salsa mixture.
7. Serve with optional toppings such as avocado slices, Greek yogurt, and lime wedges.

Nutritional Information per serving:
Cal: 290 | Fat: 1g | Chol: 0mg | Sodium: 480mg | Carbs: 63g | Fiber: 13g | Sugars: 9g | Protein: 11g

BLACK BEAN AND CORN QUESADILLAS

Yield: 4 servings | Prep time: 10 minutes | Cook time: 10 minutes

Ingredients:
- 8 whole grain tortillas
- 1 can (15 ounces) black beans, rinsed and drained
- 1 cup frozen corn, thawed
- 1 cup shredded reduced-fat cheese (such as cheddar or Monterey Jack)
- 1 teaspoon ground cumin
- 1/2 teaspoon chili powder
- Salt and pepper to taste
- Cooking spray

Directions:
1. In a medium bowl, mix together black beans, corn, shredded cheese, ground cumin, chili powder, salt, and pepper.
2. Heat a large skillet over medium heat and coat with cooking spray.
3. Place one tortilla in the skillet and spread an even layer of the black bean and corn mixture on half of the tortilla.
4. Fold the other half of the tortilla over the filling to create a half-moon shape.
5. Cook for 2-3 minutes on each side, or until the tortilla is golden brown and crispy.
6. Repeat with the remaining tortillas and filling.
7. Slice quesadillas into wedges and serve hot.

Nutritional Information per serving:
Cal: 320 | Fat: 7g | Chol: 10mg | Sodium: 490mg | Carbs: 52g | Fiber: 10g | Sugars: 3g | Protein: 15g

RATATOUILLE WITH HERBED COUSCOUS

Yield: 4 servings | Prep time: 15 minutes | Cook time: 30 minutes

Ingredients:
- 1 eggplant, diced
- 2 zucchinis, diced
- 1 yellow bell pepper, diced
- 1 red bell pepper, diced
- 1 onion, diced
- 2 cloves garlic, minced
- 1 can (15 ounces) diced tomatoes
- 2 tablespoons tomato paste
- 1 teaspoon dried thyme
- 1 teaspoon dried oregano
- Salt and pepper to taste
- 1 cup whole wheat couscous
- 1 1/4 cups vegetable broth
- 2 tablespoons chopped fresh parsley

Directions:
1. Heat olive oil in a large skillet or Dutch oven over medium heat.
2. Add diced eggplant, diced zucchinis, diced bell peppers, diced onion, and minced garlic to the skillet. Cook until vegetables are softened, about 8-10 minutes.
3. Stir in diced tomatoes, tomato paste, dried thyme, dried oregano, salt, and pepper. Simmer for 10-15 minutes, stirring occasionally.
4. In a separate saucepan, bring vegetable broth to a boil. Stir in couscous, cover, and remove from heat. Let stand for 5 minutes, then fluff with a fork.
5. Serve ratatouille over herbed couscous, garnished with chopped fresh parsley.

Nutritional Information per serving:
Cal: 290 | Fat: 1g | Chol: 0mg | Sodium: 670mg | Carbs: 62g | Fiber: 11g | Sugars: 13g | Protein: 10g

TERIYAKI TOFU STIR-FRY

Yield: 4 servings | Prep time: 10 minutes | Cook time: 15 minutes

Ingredients:
- 1 block (14 ounces) extra-firm tofu, drained and cubed
- 1/4 cup low-sodium soy sauce
- 2 tablespoons honey
- 2 cloves garlic, minced
- 1 teaspoon grated fresh ginger
- 2 tablespoons olive oil
- 1 red bell pepper, sliced
- 1 yellow bell pepper, sliced
- 1 cup broccoli florets
- 1 cup snap peas
- Cooked brown rice for serving
- Sesame seeds for garnish

Directions:
1. In a small bowl, whisk together low-sodium soy sauce, honey, minced garlic, and grated ginger to make the teriyaki sauce.
2. Heat olive oil in a large skillet or wok over medium-high heat.
3. Add cubed tofu to the skillet and cook until golden brown on all sides, about 5-7 minutes.
4. Remove tofu from the skillet and set aside.
5. In the same skillet, add sliced bell peppers, broccoli florets, and snap peas. Cook until vegetables are tender-crisp, about 5 minutes.
6. Return cooked tofu to the skillet and pour the teriyaki sauce over the tofu and vegetables. Stir to coat evenly.
7. Cook for an additional 2-3 minutes until heated through.
8. Serve teriyaki tofu stir-fry over cooked brown rice, garnished with sesame seeds.

Nutritional Information per serving:
Cal: 320 | Fat: 14g | Chol: 0mg | Sodium: 520mg | Carbs: 35g | Fiber: 5g | Sugars: 12g | Protein: 16g

STUFFED PORTOBELLO MUSHROOMS

Yield: 4 servings | Prep time: 15 minutes | Cook time: 20 minutes

Ingredients:
- 4 large portobello mushrooms, stems removed
- 1 cup cooked quinoa
- 1 can (15 ounces) black beans, rinsed and drained
- 1 cup diced tomatoes
- 1/2 cup diced red onion
- 1/4 cup chopped fresh parsley
- 2 cloves garlic, minced
- 1 teaspoon ground cumin
- 1 teaspoon chili powder
- Salt and pepper to taste
- 1/2 cup shredded reduced-fat cheese (optional)

Directions:
1. Preheat oven to 375°F (190°C). Grease a baking dish with olive oil.
2. Place portobello mushrooms on the prepared baking dish, gill side up.
3. In a large bowl, combine cooked quinoa, black beans, diced tomatoes, diced red onion, chopped fresh parsley, minced garlic, ground cumin, chili powder, salt, and pepper.
4. Spoon the quinoa and black bean mixture into each portobello mushroom cap.
5. If desired, sprinkle shredded reduced-fat cheese over the top of each stuffed mushroom.
6. Bake for 20-25 minutes until mushrooms are tender and cheese is melted.
7. Serve the stuffed portobello mushrooms hot.

Nutritional Information per serving:
Cal: 280 | Fat: 5g | Chol: 0mg | Sodium: 490mg | Carbs: 48g | Fiber: 11g | Sugars: 5g | Protein: 14g

BAKED COD WITH TOMATO AND OLIVE RELISH

Yield: 4 servings | Prep time: 10 minutes | Cook time: 20 minutes

Ingredients:
- 4 cod fillets (about 6 ounces each)
- 2 tablespoons olive oil
- 2 cloves garlic, minced
- 1 cup cherry tomatoes, halved
- 1/4 cup sliced Kalamata olives
- 2 tablespoons chopped fresh parsley
- 1 tablespoon lemon juice
- Salt and pepper to taste

Directions:
1. Preheat oven to 400°F (200°C).
2. Place cod fillets on a greased baking sheet.
3. In a small bowl, mix together olive oil, minced garlic, cherry tomatoes, Kalamata olives, chopped parsley, lemon juice, salt, and pepper.
4. Spoon the tomato and olive relish over the cod fillets.
5. Bake for 15-20 minutes until the cod is cooked through and flakes easily with a fork.
6. Serve the baked cod with tomato and olive relish hot.

Nutritional Information per serving:
Cal: 250 | Fat: 12g | Chol: 50mg | Sodium: 370mg | Carbs: 5g | Fiber: 1g | Sugars: 2g | Protein: 30g

SPAGHETTI SQUASH WITH MARINARA SAUCE

Yield: 4 servings | Prep time: 10 minutes | Cook time: 40 minutes

Ingredients:

- 1 medium spaghetti squash
- 2 cups marinara sauce (homemade or store-bought)
- 1/4 cup grated Parmesan cheese
- Fresh basil leaves for garnish

Directions:

1. Preheat oven to 400°F (200°C).
2. Cut the spaghetti squash in half lengthwise and scoop out the seeds.
3. Place the squash halves cut side down on a baking sheet lined with parchment paper.
4. Bake for 30-40 minutes, or until the squash is tender and easily pierced with a fork.
5. Use a fork to scrape the flesh of the squash into strands.
6. Heat the marinara sauce in a saucepan over medium heat until warmed through.
7. Divide the spaghetti squash strands among plates and top with marinara sauce.
8. Sprinkle with grated Parmesan cheese and garnish with fresh basil leaves.
9. Serve the spaghetti squash with marinara sauce hot.

Nutritional Information per serving:

Cal: 180 | Fat: 6g | Chol: 5mg | Sodium: 550mg | Carbs: 26g | Fiber: 6g | Sugars: 12g | Protein: 5g

TURKEY MEATBALLS IN MARINARA SAUCE

Yield: 4 servings | Prep time: 15 minutes | Cook time: 25 minutes

Ingredients:

- 1 pound ground turkey
- 1/4 cup whole wheat bread crumbs
- 1/4 cup grated Parmesan cheese
- 1 egg
- 2 cloves garlic, minced
- 1 teaspoon dried basil
- 1 teaspoon dried oregano
- Salt and pepper to taste
- 2 cups marinara sauce (homemade or store-bought)
- Fresh parsley for garnish

Directions:

1. Preheat oven to 375°F (190°C).
2. In a large bowl, combine ground turkey, bread crumbs, Parmesan cheese, egg, minced garlic, dried basil, dried oregano, salt, and pepper. Mix until well combined.
3. Shape the mixture into meatballs and place them on a greased baking sheet.
4. Bake for 20-25 minutes, or until meatballs are cooked through.
5. Meanwhile, heat the marinara sauce in a saucepan over medium heat until warmed through.
6. Serve the turkey meatballs with marinara sauce, garnished with fresh parsley.

Nutritional Information per serving:

Cal: 280 | Fat: 12g | Chol: 105mg | Sodium: 770mg | Carbs: 14g | Fiber: 2g | Sugars: 6g | Protein: 28g

VEGETABLE AND LENTIL CURRY

Yield: 4 servings | Prep time: 15 minutes | Cook time: 30 minutes

Ingredients:
- 1 tablespoon olive oil
- 1 onion, chopped
- 2 cloves garlic, minced
- 1 tablespoon curry powder
- 1 teaspoon ground turmeric
- 1 teaspoon ground cumin
- 1 cup dry red lentils, rinsed
- 1 can (15 ounces) diced tomatoes
- 2 cups vegetable broth
- 2 cups chopped mixed vegetables (such as carrots, bell peppers, and zucchini)
- Salt and pepper to taste
- Fresh cilantro for garnish

Directions:
1. Heat olive oil in a large pot over medium heat.
2. Add chopped onion and minced garlic to the pot. Cook until softened, about 5 minutes.
3. Stir in curry powder, ground turmeric, and ground cumin. Cook for 1 minute until fragrant.
4. Add dry red lentils, diced tomatoes, vegetable broth, and chopped mixed vegetables to the pot. Bring to a boil.
5. Reduce heat to low, cover, and simmer for 20-25 minutes, or until lentils and vegetables are tender.
6. Season with salt and pepper to taste.
7. Serve the vegetable and lentil curry hot, garnished with fresh cilantro.

Nutritional Information per serving:
Cal: 290 | Fat: 4g | Chol: 0mg | Sodium: 670mg | Carbs: 50g | Fiber: 15g | Sugars: 9g | Protein: 16g

EGGPLANT PARMESAN

Yield: 4 servings | Prep time: 20 minutes | Cook time: 40 minutes

Ingredients:
- 1 large eggplant, sliced into 1/2-inch rounds
- 1 cup whole wheat breadcrumbs
- 1/2 cup grated Parmesan cheese
- 1 teaspoon dried oregano
- 1 teaspoon dried basil
- Salt and pepper to taste
- 2 eggs, beaten
- 2 cups marinara sauce (homemade or store-bought)
- 1 cup shredded mozzarella cheese
- Fresh basil leaves for garnish

Directions:
1. Preheat oven to 375°F (190°C).
2. In a shallow dish, combine whole wheat breadcrumbs, grated Parmesan cheese, dried oregano, dried basil, salt, and pepper.
3. Dip eggplant slices into beaten eggs, then dredge in the breadcrumb mixture, pressing to adhere.
4. Place breaded eggplant slices on a greased baking sheet and bake for 20-25 minutes, or until golden brown and crispy.
5. In a greased baking dish, spread a thin layer of marinara sauce.
6. Arrange half of the baked eggplant slices in the baking dish, overlapping slightly.
7. Top with half of the remaining marinara sauce and half of the shredded mozzarella cheese.
8. Repeat layers with the remaining eggplant slices, marinara sauce, and mozzarella cheese.
9. Bake for 20-25 minutes, or until the cheese is melted and bubbly.
10. Garnish with fresh basil leaves before serving.

Nutritional Information per serving:
Cal: 320 | Fat: 13g | Chol: 115mg | Sodium: 690mg | Carbs: 35g | Fiber: 10g | Sugars: 8g | Protein: 18g

ITALIAN WEDDING SOUP

Yield: 6 servings | Prep time: 15 minutes | Cook time: 30 minutes

Ingredients:
- 1 tablespoon olive oil
- 1 onion, diced
- 2 carrots, diced
- 2 celery stalks, diced
- 2 cloves garlic, minced
- 6 cups low-sodium chicken or vegetable broth
- 1 cup small pasta (such as orzo or acini di pepe)
- 1 pound lean ground turkey or chicken
- 1/4 cup breadcrumbs
- 1/4 cup grated Parmesan cheese
- 1 egg, beaten
- 2 cups chopped fresh spinach or kale
- Salt and pepper to taste
- Fresh parsley for garnish

Directions:
1. In a large pot, heat olive oil over medium heat. Add diced onion, carrots, celery, and minced garlic. Cook until vegetables are softened, about 5 minutes.
2. Pour in chicken or vegetable broth and bring to a boil.
3. Stir in small pasta and cook according to package instructions until al dente.
4. Meanwhile, in a bowl, combine ground turkey or chicken, breadcrumbs, grated Parmesan cheese, beaten egg, salt, and pepper. Shape the mixture into small meatballs.
5. Drop meatballs into the simmering soup and cook for 8-10 minutes, or until meatballs are cooked through.
6. Stir in chopped fresh spinach or kale and cook for an additional 2-3 minutes until wilted.
7. Adjust seasoning with salt and pepper to taste.
8. Serve hot, garnished with fresh parsley.

Nutritional Information per serving:
Cal: 320 | Fat: 10g | Chol: 70mg | Sodium: 480mg | Carbs: 32g | Fiber: 4g | Sugars: 5g | Protein: 25g

MUSHROOM SOUP

Yield: 4 servings | Prep time: 10 minutes | Cook time: 25 minutes

Ingredients:
- 2 tablespoons olive oil
- 1 onion, chopped
- 2 cloves garlic, minced
- 1 pound mushrooms, sliced
- 4 cups low-sodium vegetable broth
- 1 teaspoon dried thyme
- Salt and pepper to taste
- 1/2 cup Greek yogurt (optional, for creamy texture)
- Fresh parsley for garnish

Directions:
1. Heat olive oil in a large pot over medium heat. Add chopped onion and minced garlic. Cook until softened, about 5 minutes.
2. Add sliced mushrooms to the pot and cook until they release their juices and become tender, about 8-10 minutes.
3. Pour in low-sodium vegetable broth and add dried thyme. Bring to a simmer and cook for another 10 minutes.
4. Use an immersion blender to puree the soup until smooth. Alternatively, transfer the soup in batches to a blender and blend until smooth, then return to the pot.
5. If desired, stir in Greek yogurt for a creamy texture.
6. Season with salt and pepper to taste.
7. Serve the mushroom soup hot, garnished with fresh parsley.

Nutritional Information per serving:
Cal: 180 | Fat: 10g | Chol: 0mg | Sodium: 430mg | Carbs: 15g | Fiber: 3g | Sugars: 6g | Protein: 7g

CHICKEN AND VEGETABLE SOUP

Yield: 6 servings | Prep time: 15 minutes | Cook time: 30 minutes

Ingredients:

- 1 tablespoon olive oil
- 1 onion, diced
- 2 carrots, diced
- 2 celery stalks, diced
- 2 cloves garlic, minced
- 6 cups low-sodium chicken broth
- 2 cups cooked shredded chicken breast
- 1 cup chopped green beans
- 1 cup diced zucchini
- 1 cup diced tomatoes
- 1 teaspoon dried thyme
- Salt and pepper to taste
- Fresh parsley for garnish

Directions:

1. In a large pot, heat olive oil over medium heat. Add diced onion, carrots, celery, and minced garlic. Cook until vegetables are softened, about 5 minutes.
2. Pour in low-sodium chicken broth and bring to a boil.
3. Stir in cooked shredded chicken breast, chopped green beans, diced zucchini, diced tomatoes, and dried thyme. Simmer for 15-20 minutes until vegetables are tender.
4. Season with salt and pepper to taste.
5. Serve the chicken and vegetable soup hot, garnished with fresh parsley.

Nutritional Information per serving:

Cal: 180 | Fat: 5g | Chol: 35mg | Sodium: 590mg | Carbs: 12g | Fiber: 3g | Sugars: 5g | Protein: 20g

SPLIT PEA SOUP

Yield: 6 servings | Prep time: 10 minutes | Cook time: 1 hour 30 minutes

Ingredients:

- 1 tablespoon olive oil
- 1 onion, diced
- 2 carrots, diced
- 2 celery stalks, diced
- 2 cloves garlic, minced
- 1 pound dried split peas, rinsed and drained
- 8 cups low-sodium vegetable broth
- 1 bay leaf
- 1 teaspoon dried thyme
- Salt and pepper to taste
- Fresh parsley for garnish

Directions:

1. In a large pot, heat olive oil over medium heat. Add diced onion, carrots, celery, and minced garlic. Cook until vegetables are softened, about 5 minutes.
2. Add dried split peas to the pot and stir to combine.
3. Pour in low-sodium vegetable broth and add bay leaf and dried thyme. Bring to a boil, then reduce heat to low and simmer, covered, for 1 hour.
4. Remove the bay leaf from the soup.
5. Use an immersion blender to puree the soup until smooth. Alternatively, transfer the soup in batches to a blender and blend until smooth, then return to the pot.
6. Season with salt and pepper to taste.
7. Serve the split pea soup hot, garnished with fresh parsley.

Nutritional Information per serving:

Cal: 260 | Fat: 2.5g | Chol: 0mg | Sodium: 450mg | Carbs: 45g | Fiber: 16g | Sugars: 8g | Protein: 17g

BROCCOLI CHEDDAR SOUP

Yield: 4 servings | Prep time: 10 minutes | Cook time: 25 minutes

Ingredients:
- 1 tablespoon olive oil
- 1 onion, chopped
- 2 cloves garlic, minced
- 2 cups chopped broccoli florets
- 4 cups low-sodium vegetable broth
- 1 cup low-fat milk or unsweetened almond milk
- 1 cup shredded reduced-fat cheddar cheese
- 2 tablespoons whole wheat flour
- Salt and pepper to taste

Directions:
1. In a large pot, heat olive oil over medium heat. Add chopped onion and minced garlic. Cook until softened, about 5 minutes.
2. Add chopped broccoli florets to the pot and cook for another 3-4 minutes.
3. Pour in low-sodium vegetable broth and bring to a boil. Reduce heat to low and simmer for 10-15 minutes until broccoli is tender.
4. In a small bowl, whisk together low-fat milk or unsweetened almond milk and whole wheat flour until smooth.
5. Gradually pour the milk mixture into the soup, stirring constantly. Cook for 3-4 minutes until slightly thickened.
6. Stir in shredded reduced-fat cheddar cheese until melted and smooth.
7. Season with salt and pepper to taste.
8. Serve the broccoli cheddar soup hot.

Nutritional Information per serving:
Cal: 240 | Fat: 10g | Chol: 15mg | Sodium: 570mg | Carbs: 25g | Fiber: 5g | Sugars: 8g | Protein: 14g

BUTTERNUT SQUASH SOUP

Yield: 4 servings | Prep time: 15 minutes | Cook time: 40 minutes

Ingredients:
- 1 tablespoon olive oil
- 1 onion, chopped
- 2 cloves garlic, minced
- 1 butternut squash, peeled, seeded, and cubed
- 4 cups low-sodium vegetable broth
- 1 teaspoon dried thyme
- 1/2 teaspoon ground cinnamon
- Salt and pepper to taste
- Optional toppings: Greek yogurt, pumpkin seeds, fresh thyme

Directions:
1. In a large pot, heat olive oil over medium heat. Add chopped onion and minced garlic. Cook until softened, about 5 minutes.
2. Add cubed butternut squash to the pot and cook for another 5 minutes.
3. Pour in low-sodium vegetable broth and add dried thyme and ground cinnamon. Bring to a boil, then reduce heat to low and simmer for 25-30 minutes until squash is tender.
4. Use an immersion blender to puree the soup until smooth. Alternatively, transfer the soup in batches to a blender and blend until smooth, then return to the pot.
5. Season with salt and pepper to taste.
6. Serve the butternut squash soup hot, topped with optional toppings if desired.

Nutritional Information per serving:
Cal: 160 | Fat: 3.5g | Chol: 0mg | Sodium: 480mg | Carbs: 32g | Fiber: 7g | Sugars: 7g | Protein: 3g

TOMATO BASIL SOUP

Yield: 4 servings | Prep time: 10 minutes | Cook time: 25 minutes

Ingredients:

- 1 tablespoon olive oil
- 1 onion, chopped
- 2 cloves garlic, minced
- 1 can (28 ounces) diced tomatoes
- 2 cups low-sodium vegetable broth
- 1/4 cup chopped fresh basil leaves
- Salt and pepper to taste
- Optional toppings: Greek yogurt, fresh basil leaves, croutons

Directions:

1. In a large pot, heat olive oil over medium heat. Add chopped onion and minced garlic. Cook until softened, about 5 minutes.
2. Add diced tomatoes (with their juices) to the pot and stir to combine.
3. Pour in low-sodium vegetable broth and bring to a simmer. Cook for 15-20 minutes.
4. Stir in chopped fresh basil leaves and cook for an additional 2-3 minutes.
5. Use an immersion blender to puree the soup until smooth. Alternatively, transfer the soup in batches to a blender and blend until smooth, then return to the pot.
6. Season with salt and pepper to taste.
7. Serve the tomato basil soup hot, topped with optional toppings if desired.

Nutritional Information per serving:

Cal: 90 | Fat: 3g | Chol: 0mg | Sodium: 470mg | Carbs: 14g | Fiber: 3g | Sugars: 7g | Protein: 3g

SPINACH AND WHITE BEAN SOUP

Yield: 4 servings | Prep time: 10 minutes | Cook time: 25 minutes

Ingredients:

- 1 tablespoon olive oil
- 1 onion, chopped
- 2 cloves garlic, minced
- 4 cups low-sodium vegetable broth
- 1 can (15 ounces) white beans, rinsed and drained
- 2 cups chopped fresh spinach
- 1 teaspoon dried oregano
- Salt and pepper to taste
- Optional toppings: grated Parmesan cheese, lemon wedges, chopped fresh parsley

Directions:

1. In a large pot, heat olive oil over medium heat. Add chopped onion and minced garlic. Cook until softened, about 5 minutes.
2. Pour in low-sodium vegetable broth and bring to a simmer.
3. Stir in white beans, chopped fresh spinach, and dried oregano. Cook for 10-15 minutes until spinach is wilted.
4. Use an immersion blender to partially puree the soup, leaving some beans and spinach whole. Alternatively, mash some of the beans with a fork or potato masher to thicken the soup.
5. Season with salt and pepper to taste.
6. Serve the spinach and white bean soup hot, topped with optional toppings if desired.

Nutritional Information per serving:

Cal: 150 | Fat: 3.5g | Chol: 0mg | Sodium: 630mg | Carbs: 23g | Fiber: 7g | Sugars: 2g | Protein: 8g

MOROCCAN CHICKPEA SOUP

Yield: 4 servings | Prep time: 15 minutes | Cook time: 30 minutes

Ingredients:
- 1 tablespoon olive oil
- 1 onion, chopped
- 2 cloves garlic, minced
- 1 teaspoon ground cumin
- 1 teaspoon ground coriander
- 1/2 teaspoon ground cinnamon
- 1/4 teaspoon ground turmeric
- 4 cups low-sodium vegetable broth
- 1 can (15 ounces) chickpeas, rinsed and drained
- 1 can (14 ounces) diced tomatoes
- 1 cup chopped carrots
- 1/4 cup chopped fresh cilantro
- Salt and pepper to taste
- Optional toppings: Greek yogurt, chopped fresh mint, lemon wedges

Directions:
1. In a large pot, heat olive oil over medium heat. Add chopped onion and minced garlic. Cook until softened, about 5 minutes.
2. Stir in ground cumin, ground coriander, ground cinnamon, and ground turmeric. Cook for 1 minute until fragrant.
3. Pour in low-sodium vegetable broth and bring to a boil.
4. Add chickpeas, diced tomatoes, and chopped carrots to the pot. Simmer for 15-20 minutes until carrots are tender.
5. Stir in chopped fresh cilantro and cook for an additional 2-3 minutes.
6. Season with salt and pepper to taste.
7. Serve the Moroccan chickpea soup hot, topped with optional toppings if desired.

Nutritional Information per serving:
Cal: 210 | Fat: 5g | Chol: 0mg | Sodium: 690mg | Carbs: 34g | Fiber: 8g | Sugars: 8g | Protein: 9g

VEGETABLE BARLEY SOUP

Yield: 6 servings | Prep time: 15 minutes | Cook time: 40 minutes

Ingredients:
- 1 tablespoon olive oil
- 1 onion, chopped
- 2 cloves garlic, minced
- 2 carrots, diced
- 2 celery stalks, diced
- 1 cup pearl barley
- 6 cups low-sodium vegetable broth
- 1 can (15 ounces) diced tomatoes
- 1 teaspoon dried thyme
- Salt and pepper to taste
- Fresh parsley for garnish

Directions:
1. In a large pot, heat olive oil over medium heat. Add chopped onion and minced garlic. Cook until softened, about 5 minutes.
2. Add diced carrots and celery to the pot. Cook for another 5 minutes.
3. Stir in pearl barley and cook for 2-3 minutes.
4. Pour in low-sodium vegetable broth and add diced tomatoes (with their juices) and dried thyme. Bring to a boil, then reduce heat to low and simmer for 30-35 minutes until barley is tender.
5. Season with salt and pepper to taste.
6. Serve the vegetable barley soup hot, garnished with fresh parsley.

Nutritional Information per serving:
Cal: 230 | Fat: 3.5g | Chol: 0mg | Sodium: 720mg | Carbs: 46g | Fiber: 9g | Sugars: 7g | Protein: 6g

Chapter 6
MEAT & POULTRY

BAKED GARLIC PARMESAN CHICKEN

Yield: 4 servings | Prep time: 10 minutes | Cook time: 25 minutes

Ingredients:
- 4 boneless, skinless chicken breasts
- 1/2 cup grated Parmesan cheese
- 1/4 cup whole wheat breadcrumbs
- 2 cloves garlic, minced
- 1 teaspoon dried oregano
- 1 teaspoon dried basil
- Salt and pepper to taste
- Cooking spray

Directions:
1. Preheat oven to 400°F (200°C). Grease a baking dish with cooking spray.
2. In a small bowl, combine grated Parmesan cheese, whole wheat breadcrumbs, minced garlic, dried oregano, dried basil, salt, and pepper.
3. Pat chicken breasts dry with paper towels and place them in the prepared baking dish.
4. Sprinkle the Parmesan mixture evenly over the chicken breasts, pressing gently to adhere.
5. Bake for 20-25 minutes, or until chicken is cooked through and juices run clear.
6. Serve the baked garlic Parmesan chicken hot, garnished with fresh parsley if desired.

Nutritional Information per serving:
Cal: 250 | Fat: 7g | Chol: 90mg | Sodium: 370mg | Carbs: 7g | Fiber: 1g | Sugars: 1g | Protein: 38g

TURKEY MEATLOAF WITH TOMATO GLAZE

Yield: 6 servings | Prep time: 15 minutes | Cook time: 1 hour

Ingredients:
- 1 pound ground turkey
- 1/2 cup whole wheat breadcrumbs
- 1/4 cup grated Parmesan cheese
- 1/4 cup chopped onion
- 1/4 cup chopped bell pepper
- 1 egg, beaten
- 2 cloves garlic, minced
- 1 teaspoon dried oregano
- Salt and pepper to taste
- 1/2 cup tomato sauce
- 2 tablespoons honey
- 1 tablespoon balsamic vinegar

Directions:
1. Preheat oven to 375°F (190°C). Grease a loaf pan with cooking spray.
2. In a large bowl, combine ground turkey, whole wheat breadcrumbs, grated Parmesan cheese, chopped onion, chopped bell pepper, beaten egg, minced garlic, dried oregano, salt, and pepper. Mix until well combined.
3. Transfer the turkey mixture to the prepared loaf pan and shape into a loaf.
4. In a small bowl, whisk together tomato sauce, honey, and balsamic vinegar. Pour the glaze over the meatloaf, spreading evenly.
5. Bake for 50-60 minutes, or until meatloaf is cooked through and internal temperature reaches 165°F (75°C).
6. Let the turkey meatloaf rest for 10 minutes before slicing.
7. Serve the turkey meatloaf with tomato glaze hot, garnished with fresh parsley if desired.

Nutritional Information per serving:
Cal: 230 | Fat: 8g | Chol: 80mg | Sodium: 370mg | Carbs: 17g | Fiber: 2g | Sugars: 9g | Protein: 21g

MEDITERRANEAN STUFFED CHICKEN BREASTS

Yield: 4 servings | Prep time: 20 minutes | Cook time: 25 minutes

Ingredients:

- 4 boneless, skinless chicken breasts
- 1/2 cup chopped sun-dried tomatoes
- 1/4 cup chopped Kalamata olives
- 1/4 cup crumbled feta cheese
- 2 tablespoons chopped fresh basil
- 1 tablespoon olive oil
- 2 cloves garlic, minced
- Salt and pepper to taste
- Toothpicks

Directions:

1. Preheat oven to 375°F (190°C). Grease a baking dish with cooking spray.
2. In a small bowl, combine chopped sun-dried tomatoes, chopped Kalamata olives, crumbled feta cheese, chopped fresh basil, olive oil, minced garlic, salt, and pepper.
3. Using a sharp knife, cut a slit horizontally along the side of each chicken breast to create a pocket, being careful not to cut all the way through.
4. Stuff each chicken breast with the Mediterranean filling mixture, then secure the openings with toothpicks.
5. Place stuffed chicken breasts in the prepared baking dish.
6. Bake for 20-25 minutes, or until chicken is cooked through and juices run clear.
7. Serve the Mediterranean stuffed chicken breasts hot, removing toothpicks before serving.

Nutritional Information per serving:

Cal: 280 | Fat: 10g | Chol: 90mg | Sodium: 370mg | Carbs: 8g | Fiber: 2g | Sugars: 4g | Protein: 38g

HERB-MARINATED GRILLED STEAK

Yield: 4 servings | Prep time: 15 minutes (plus marinating time) | Cook time: 10 minutes

Ingredients:

- 1 pound flank steak
- 2 tablespoons olive oil
- 2 cloves garlic, minced
- 2 tablespoons chopped fresh parsley
- 1 tablespoon chopped fresh thyme
- 1 tablespoon chopped fresh rosemary
- 1 tablespoon balsamic vinegar
- Salt and pepper to taste

Directions:

1. In a small bowl, whisk together olive oil, minced garlic, chopped fresh parsley, chopped fresh thyme, chopped fresh rosemary, balsamic vinegar, salt, and pepper to make the marinade.
2. Place flank steak in a shallow dish or resealable plastic bag. Pour the marinade over the steak, turning to coat evenly. Cover or seal and refrigerate for at least 2 hours, or overnight for best flavor.
3. Preheat grill to medium-high heat.
4. Remove steak from marinade and discard excess marinade.
5. Grill steak for 4-5 minutes per side, or until desired doneness is reached.
6. Transfer grilled steak to a cutting board and let rest for 5 minutes before slicing thinly against the grain.
7. Serve the herb-marinated grilled steak hot, garnished with additional chopped fresh herbs if desired.

Nutritional Information per serving:

Cal: 280 | Fat: 16g | Chol: 75mg | Sodium: 75mg | Carbs: 1g | Fiber: 0g | Sugars: 0g | Protein: 29g

BALSAMIC GLAZED PORK CHOPS

Yield: 4 servings | Prep time: 10 minutes | Cook time: 20 minutes

Ingredients:
- 4 boneless pork chops
- 1/4 cup balsamic vinegar
- 2 tablespoons honey
- 2 cloves garlic, minced
- 1 teaspoon dried rosemary
- Salt and pepper to taste
- Cooking spray

Directions:
1. In a small bowl, whisk together balsamic vinegar, honey, minced garlic, dried rosemary, salt, and pepper to make the glaze.
2. Season pork chops with salt and pepper on both sides.
3. Preheat grill or grill pan over medium-high heat and grease with cooking spray.
4. Place pork chops on the grill and cook for 6-8 minutes per side, or until internal temperature reaches 145°F (63°C), basting with the balsamic glaze during the last few minutes of cooking.
5. Remove pork chops from the grill and let rest for 5 minutes before serving.
6. Serve the balsamic glazed pork chops hot, drizzled with any remaining glaze.

Nutritional Information per serving:
Cal: 230 | Fat: 9g | Chol: 65mg | Sodium: 60mg | Carbs: 9g | Fiber: 0g | Sugars: 9g | Protein: 26g

HONEY MUSTARD GLAZED CHICKEN THIGHS

Yield: 4 servings | Prep time: 10 minutes | Cook time: 25 minutes

Ingredients:
- 4 bone-in, skinless chicken thighs
- 1/4 cup Dijon mustard
- 2 tablespoons honey
- 1 tablespoon olive oil
- 2 cloves garlic, minced
- Salt and pepper to taste

Directions:
1. Preheat oven to 400°F (200°C). Grease a baking dish with cooking spray.
2. Season chicken thighs with salt and pepper on both sides.
3. In a small bowl, whisk together Dijon mustard, honey, olive oil, and minced garlic to make the glaze.
4. Place chicken thighs in the prepared baking dish and brush with half of the honey mustard glaze.
5. Bake for 20-25 minutes, or until chicken is cooked through and juices run clear, brushing with the remaining glaze halfway through cooking.
6. Serve the honey mustard glazed chicken thighs hot.

Nutritional Information per serving:
Cal: 260 | Fat: 14g | Chol: 110mg | Sodium: 240mg | Carbs: Carbs: 11g | Fiber: 0g | Sugars: 9g | Protein: 20g

GREEK STYLE GRILLED LAMB CHOPS

Yield: 4 servings | Prep time: 10 minutes (plus marinating time) | Cook time: 10 minutes

Ingredients:
- 8 lamb loin chops
- 1/4 cup olive oil
- 2 cloves garlic, minced
- 1 tablespoon dried oregano
- 1 teaspoon dried thyme
- 1/2 teaspoon dried rosemary
- Juice of 1 lemon
- Salt and pepper to taste

Directions:
1. In a small bowl, whisk together olive oil, minced garlic, dried oregano, dried thyme, dried rosemary, lemon juice, salt, and pepper to make the marinade.
2. Place lamb chops in a shallow dish or resealable plastic bag. Pour the marinade over the lamb chops, turning to coat evenly. Cover or seal and refrigerate for at least 2 hours, or overnight for best flavor.
3. Preheat grill to medium-high heat.
4. Remove lamb chops from marinade and discard excess marinade.
5. Grill lamb chops for 3-4 minutes per side, or until desired doneness is reached.
6. Transfer grilled lamb chops to a serving platter and let rest for 5 minutes before serving.
7. Serve the Greek style grilled lamb chops hot, garnished with fresh parsley if desired.

Nutritional Information per serving:
Cal: 320 | Fat: 24g | Chol: 80mg | Sodium: 60mg | Carbs: 1g | Fiber: 0g | Sugars: 0g | Protein: 25g

PESTO TURKEY MEATBALLS

Yield: 4 servings | Prep time: 15 minutes | Cook time: 20 minutes

Ingredients:
- 1 pound ground turkey
- 1/4 cup whole wheat breadcrumbs
- 1/4 cup grated Parmesan cheese
- 2 tablespoons prepared pesto
- 1 egg, beaten
- 2 cloves garlic, minced
- Salt and pepper to taste
- Cooking spray

Directions:
1. Preheat oven to 400°F (200°C). Line a baking sheet with parchment paper and grease with cooking spray.
2. In a large bowl, combine ground turkey, whole wheat breadcrumbs, grated Parmesan cheese, prepared pesto, beaten egg, minced garlic, salt, and pepper. Mix until well combined.
3. Shape the turkey mixture into meatballs and place them on the prepared baking sheet.
4. Bake for 18-20 minutes, or until meatballs are cooked through and golden brown.
5. Serve the pesto turkey meatballs hot, garnished with fresh basil if desired.

Nutritional Information per serving:
Cal: 250 | Fat: 14g | Chol: 100mg | Sodium: 250mg | Carbs: 6g | Fiber: 1g | Sugars: 1g | Protein: 24g

ORANGE GLAZED GRILLED CHICKEN

Yield: 4 servings | Prep time: 10 minutes (plus marinating time) | Cook time: 15 minutes

Ingredients:
- 4 boneless, skinless chicken breasts
- 1/4 cup orange juice
- Zest of 1 orange
- 2 tablespoons honey
- 2 cloves garlic, minced
- 1 tablespoon soy sauce
- Salt and pepper to taste

Directions:
1. In a small bowl, whisk together orange juice, orange zest, honey, minced garlic, soy sauce, salt, and pepper to make the marinade.
2. Place chicken breasts in a shallow dish or resealable plastic bag. Pour the marinade over the chicken breasts, turning to coat evenly. Cover or seal and refrigerate for at least 30 minutes, or up to 4 hours.
3. Preheat grill to medium-high heat.
4. Remove chicken breasts from marinade and discard excess marinade.
5. Grill chicken breasts for 6-7 minutes per side, or until cooked through and juices run clear.
6. Serve the orange glazed grilled chicken hot, garnished with orange slices if desired.

Nutritional Information per serving:
Cal: 220 | Fat: 3g | Chol: 80mg | Sodium: 230mg | Carbs: 14g | Fiber: 0g | Sugars: 13g | Protein: 30g

ITALIAN HERB CRUSTED PORK TENDERLOIN

Yield: 4 servings | Prep time: 10 minutes | Cook time: 25 minutes

Ingredients:
- 1 pound pork tenderloin
- 1 tablespoon olive oil
- 2 cloves garlic, minced
- 1 tablespoon chopped fresh rosemary
- 1 tablespoon chopped fresh thyme
- 1 tablespoon chopped fresh parsley
- Salt and pepper to taste

Directions:
1. Preheat oven to 400°F (200°C). Line a baking sheet with parchment paper.
2. In a small bowl, combine olive oil, minced garlic, chopped fresh rosemary, chopped fresh thyme, chopped fresh parsley, salt, and pepper to make the herb crust.
3. Pat pork tenderloin dry with paper towels and place it on the prepared baking sheet.
4. Rub the herb crust mixture evenly over the pork tenderloin.
5. Roast pork tenderloin in the preheated oven for 20-25 minutes, or until internal temperature reaches 145°F (63°C).
6. Remove pork tenderloin from the oven and let rest for 5 minutes before slicing.
7. Serve the Italian herb-crusted pork tenderloin hot, garnished with additional chopped fresh herbs if desired.

Nutritional Information per serving:
Cal: 220 | Fat: 8g | Chol: 80mg | Sodium: 70mg | Carbs: 1g | Fiber: 0g | Sugars: 0g | Protein: 35g

Chapter 7
FISH & SEAFOOD

SPICY SRIRACHA TUNA CAKES

Yield: 4 servings | Prep time: 10 minutes | Cook time: 10 minutes

Ingredients:
- 2 cans (5 ounces each) tuna, drained
- 1/4 cup whole wheat breadcrumbs
- 2 green onions, finely chopped
- 1 egg, beaten
- 1 tablespoon Sriracha sauce
- 1 tablespoon soy sauce
- 1 tablespoon lime juice
- 1 teaspoon minced garlic
- 1 teaspoon grated ginger
- 1 tablespoon olive oil
- Salt and pepper to taste
- Cooking spray

Directions:
1. In a large bowl, combine drained tuna, whole wheat breadcrumbs, chopped green onions, beaten egg, Sriracha sauce, soy sauce, lime juice, minced garlic, grated ginger, salt, and pepper. Mix until well combined.
2. Shape the tuna mixture into patties.
3. Heat olive oil in a skillet over medium heat. Cook tuna cakes for 4-5 minutes on each side, or until golden brown and heated through.
4. Serve the spicy Sriracha tuna cakes hot, garnished with additional chopped green onions if desired.

Nutritional Information per serving:
Cal: 170 | Fat: 6g | Chol: 70mg | Sodium: 340mg | Carbs: 7g | Fiber: 1g | Sugars: 1g | Protein: 22g

BAKED DIJON TILAPIA

Yield: 4 servings | Prep time: 10 minutes | Cook time: 15 minutes

Ingredients:
- 4 tilapia fillets
- 2 tablespoons Dijon mustard
- 1 tablespoon olive oil
- 1 tablespoon lemon juice
- 1 teaspoon minced garlic
- 1 teaspoon dried parsley
- Salt and pepper to taste
- Lemon wedges for serving

Directions:
1. Preheat oven to 400°F (200°C). Grease a baking dish with cooking spray.
2. In a small bowl, whisk together Dijon mustard, olive oil, lemon juice, minced garlic, dried parsley, salt, and pepper.
3. Place tilapia fillets in the prepared baking dish. Brush the Dijon mustard mixture evenly over the tilapia fillets.
4. Bake for 12-15 minutes, or until fish flakes easily with a fork.
5. Serve the baked Dijon tilapia hot, with lemon wedges on the side.

Nutritional Information per serving:
Cal: 160 | Fat: 7g | Chol: 50mg | Sodium: 260mg | Carbs: 2g | Fiber: 0g | Sugars: 0g | Protein: 23g

SHRIMP STIR-FRY WITH VEGETABLES

Yield: 4 servings | Prep time: 15 minutes | Cook time: 10 minutes

Ingredients:

- 1 pound shrimp, peeled and deveined
- 2 cups mixed vegetables (such as bell peppers, broccoli, snap peas)
- 2 cloves garlic, minced
- 1 tablespoon grated ginger
- 2 tablespoons low-sodium soy sauce
- 1 tablespoon hoisin sauce
- 1 tablespoon rice vinegar
- 1 teaspoon sesame oil
- 1 tablespoon olive oil
- Salt and pepper to taste
- Cooked brown rice for serving

Directions:

1. Heat olive oil in a large skillet or wok over medium-high heat. Add minced garlic and grated ginger, and cook for 1 minute.
2. Add shrimp to the skillet and cook until pink and opaque, about 2-3 minutes.
3. Add mixed vegetables to the skillet and cook until tender-crisp, about 3-4 minutes.
4. In a small bowl, whisk together low-sodium soy sauce, hoisin sauce, rice vinegar, and sesame oil. Pour the sauce over the shrimp and vegetables, and toss to coat.
5. Cook for another 1-2 minutes, until heated through.
6. Serve the shrimp stir-fry with vegetables hot, over cooked brown rice.

Nutritional Information per serving:

Cal: 210 | Fat: 7g | Chol: 170mg | Sodium: 620mg | Carbs: 9g | Fiber: 2g | Sugars: 4g | Protein: 26g

TERIYAKI GLAZED MAHI MAHI

Yield: 4 servings | Prep time: 10 minutes (plus marinating time) | Cook time: 10 minutes

Ingredients:

- 4 mahi mahi fillets
- 1/4 cup low-sodium soy sauce
- 2 tablespoons honey
- 1 tablespoon rice vinegar
- 1 tablespoon olive oil
- 1 teaspoon minced garlic
- 1 teaspoon grated ginger
- 1 teaspoon cornstarch
- 2 tablespoons water
- Sesame seeds for garnish

Directions:

1. In a small bowl, whisk together low-sodium soy sauce, honey, rice vinegar, olive oil, minced garlic, and grated ginger to make the teriyaki marinade.
2. Place mahi mahi fillets in a shallow dish or resealable plastic bag. Pour the marinade over the fish fillets, turning to coat evenly. Cover or seal and refrigerate for at least 30 minutes, or up to 4 hours.
3. Preheat grill to medium-high heat.
4. Remove mahi mahi fillets from marinade and discard excess marinade.
5. Grill mahi mahi fillets for 4-5 minutes per side, or until fish flakes easily with a fork.
6. In a small bowl, whisk together cornstarch and water to make a slurry. Heat the remaining marinade in a small saucepan over medium heat. Once simmering, add the cornstarch slurry and cook until thickened, stirring constantly.
7. Brush the teriyaki glaze over the grilled mahi mahi fillets, and sprinkle with sesame seeds.
8. Serve the teriyaki glazed mahi mahi hot, garnished with additional sesame seeds if desired.

Nutritional Information per serving:

Cal: 220 | Fat: 6g | Chol: 145mg | Sodium: 340mg | Carbs: 11g | Fiber: 0g | Sugars: 9g | Protein: 30g

MEDITERRANEAN BAKED HALIBUT

Yield: 4 servings | Prep time: 10 minutes | Cook time: 15 minutes

Ingredients:
- 4 halibut fillets
- 1/4 cup chopped sun-dried tomatoes
- 1/4 cup chopped Kalamata olives
- 2 cloves garlic, minced
- 2 tablespoons chopped fresh parsley
- 1 tablespoon olive oil
- 1 tablespoon lemon juice
- Salt and pepper to taste

Directions:
1. Preheat oven to 400°F (200°C). Grease a baking dish with cooking spray.
2. In a small bowl, combine chopped sun-dried tomatoes, chopped Kalamata olives, minced garlic, chopped fresh parsley, olive oil, lemon juice, salt, and pepper.
3. Place halibut fillets in the prepared baking dish. Spread the Mediterranean mixture evenly over the halibut fillets.
4. Bake for 12-15 minutes, or until fish flakes easily with a fork.
5. Serve the Mediterranean baked halibut hot, garnished with additional chopped fresh parsley if desired.

Nutritional Information per serving:
Cal: 190 | Fat: 8g | Chol: 45mg | Sodium: 340mg | Carbs: 5g | Fiber: 1g | Sugars: 2g | Protein: 25g

GARLIC PARMESAN CRUSTED SALMON

Yield: 4 servings | Prep time: 10 minutes | Cook time: 15 minutes

Ingredients:
- 4 salmon fillets
- 1/4 cup grated Parmesan cheese
- 2 tablespoons whole wheat breadcrumbs
- 2 cloves garlic, minced
- 2 tablespoons chopped fresh parsley
- 2 tablespoons olive oil
- Salt and pepper to taste
- Lemon wedges for serving

Directions:
1. Preheat oven to 400°F (200°C). Grease a baking dish with cooking spray.
2. In a small bowl, combine grated Parmesan cheese, whole wheat breadcrumbs, minced garlic, chopped fresh parsley, olive oil, salt, and pepper.
3. Place salmon fillets in the prepared baking dish. Press the Parmesan mixture onto the top of each salmon fillet.
4. Bake for 12-15 minutes, or until salmon is cooked through and flakes easily with a fork.
5. Serve the garlic Parmesan crusted salmon hot, with lemon wedges on the side.

Nutritional Information per serving:
Cal: 290 | Fat: 16g | Chol: 80mg | Sodium: 240mg | Carbs: 3g | Fiber: 0g | Sugars: 0g | Protein: 31g

LEMON GARLIC BUTTER SCALLOPS

Yield: 4 servings | Prep time: 10 minutes | Cook time: 5 minutes

Ingredients:

- 1 pound sea scallops
- 2 tablespoons unsalted butter
- 2 cloves garlic, minced
- Zest and juice of 1 lemon
- 2 tablespoons chopped fresh parsley
- Salt and pepper to taste

Directions:

1. Pat scallops dry with paper towels and season with salt and pepper.
2. In a large skillet, melt butter over medium-high heat. Add minced garlic and cook until fragrant, about 1 minute.
3. Add scallops to the skillet and cook for 2-3 minutes per side, or until golden brown and cooked through.
4. Remove skillet from heat and stir in lemon zest, lemon juice, and chopped fresh parsley.
5. Serve the lemon garlic butter scallops hot, garnished with additional chopped parsley if desired.

Nutritional Information per serving:

Cal: 170 | Fat: 8g | Chol: 45mg | Sodium: 560mg | Carbs: 4g | Fiber: 0g | Sugars: 0g | Protein: 20g

HERB CRUSTED BAKED SNAPPER

Yield: 4 servings | Prep time: 10 minutes | Cook time: 15 minutes

Ingredients:

- 4 snapper fillets
- 2 tablespoons olive oil
- 2 cloves garlic, minced
- 2 tablespoons chopped fresh parsley
- 1 tablespoon chopped fresh thyme
- 1 tablespoon chopped fresh rosemary
- Salt and pepper to taste
- Lemon wedges for serving

Directions:

1. Preheat oven to 400°F (200°C). Grease a baking dish with cooking spray.
2. In a small bowl, combine olive oil, minced garlic, chopped fresh parsley, chopped fresh thyme, chopped fresh rosemary, salt, and pepper.
3. Place snapper fillets in the prepared baking dish. Spread the herb mixture evenly over the top of each snapper fillet.
4. Bake for 12-15 minutes, or until fish is cooked through and flakes easily with a fork.
5. Serve the herb crusted baked snapper hot, with lemon wedges on the side.

Nutritional Information per serving:

Cal: 220 | Fat: 10g | Chol: 50mg | Sodium: 300mg | Carbs: 1g | Fiber: 0g | Sugars: 0g | Protein: 28g

GARLIC BUTTER LEMON SHRIMP PASTA

Yield: 4 servings | Prep time: 10 minutes | Cook time: 15 minutes

Ingredients:
- 8 ounces whole wheat spaghetti
- 1 pound large shrimp, peeled and deveined
- 4 tablespoons unsalted butter
- 4 cloves garlic, minced
- Zest and juice of 1 lemon
- 2 tablespoons chopped fresh parsley
- Salt and pepper to taste

Directions:
1. Cook spaghetti according to package instructions. Drain and set aside.
2. In a large skillet, melt butter over medium heat. Add minced garlic and cook until fragrant, about 1 minute.
3. Add shrimp to the skillet and cook for 2-3 minutes per side, or until pink and opaque.
4. Stir in lemon zest, lemon juice, chopped fresh parsley, cooked spaghetti, salt, and pepper. Toss until well combined and heated through.
5. Serve the garlic butter lemon shrimp pasta hot, garnished with additional chopped parsley if desired.

Nutritional Information per serving:
Cal: 350 | Fat: 12g | Chol: 190mg | Sodium: 270mg | Carbs: 36g | Fiber: 6g | Sugars: 2g | Protein: 26g

BAKED LEMON HERB TROUT

Yield: 4 servings | Prep time: 10 minutes | Cook time: 15 minutes

Ingredients:
- 4 trout fillets
- 2 tablespoons olive oil
- Zest and juice of 1 lemon
- 2 cloves garlic, minced
- 2 tablespoons chopped fresh parsley
- 1 tablespoon chopped fresh dill
- Salt and pepper to taste

Directions:
1. Preheat oven to 400°F (200°C). Grease a baking dish with cooking spray.
2. In a small bowl, combine olive oil, lemon zest, lemon juice, minced garlic, chopped fresh parsley, chopped fresh dill, salt, and pepper.
3. Place trout fillets in the prepared baking dish. Spread the herb mixture evenly over the top of each trout fillet.
4. Bake for 12-15 minutes, or until fish is cooked through and flakes easily with a fork.
5. Serve the baked lemon herb trout hot, garnished with additional chopped parsley if desired.

Nutritional Information per serving:
Cal: 240 | Fat: 12g | Chol: 80mg | Sodium: 100mg | Carbs: 2g | Fiber: 0g | Sugars: 0g | Protein: 30g

TUNA NICOISE SALAD

Yield: 4 servings | Prep time: 15 minutes | Cook time: 10 minutes

Ingredients:
- 1 pound small red potatoes
- 4 eggs
- 8 ounces green beans, trimmed
- 2 cans (5 ounces each) tuna, drained
- 2 cups cherry tomatoes, halved
- 1/2 cup Kalamata olives, pitted
- 4 cups mixed salad greens
- 1/4 cup red wine vinegar
- 1/3 cup extra virgin olive oil
- 1 teaspoon Dijon mustard
- Salt and pepper to taste

Directions:
1. Place potatoes in a saucepan and cover with water. Bring to a boil, then reduce heat and simmer for 10-15 minutes, or until potatoes are fork-tender. Drain and set aside to cool.
2. Meanwhile, place eggs in a small saucepan and cover with water. Bring to a boil, then remove from heat and let eggs sit in hot water for 10-12 minutes. Transfer eggs to a bowl of ice water to cool. Peel and slice eggs.
3. Bring a pot of water to a boil. Add green beans and blanch for 2-3 minutes, then transfer to a bowl of ice water to cool. Drain and set aside.
4. In a large bowl, arrange mixed salad greens. Top with cooked potatoes, sliced eggs, green beans, tuna, cherry tomatoes, and Kalamata olives.
5. In a small bowl, whisk together red wine vinegar, extra virgin olive oil, Dijon mustard, salt, and pepper to make the dressing.
6. Drizzle dressing over the salad and toss gently to combine.
7. Serve the Tuna Nicoise Salad chilled.

Nutritional Information per serving:
Cal: 420 | Fat: 26g | Chol: 190mg | Sodium: 570mg | Carbs: 23g | Fiber: 5g | Sugars: 5g | Protein: 24g

SPINACH AND STRAWBERRY SALAD

Yield: 4 servings | Prep time: 10 minutes | Cook time: 0 minutes

Ingredients:
- 6 cups baby spinach leaves
- 2 cups sliced strawberries
- 1/4 cup sliced almonds
- 1/4 cup crumbled feta cheese
- 2 tablespoons balsamic vinegar
- 2 tablespoons extra virgin olive oil
- 1 teaspoon honey
- Salt and pepper to taste

Directions:
1. In a large bowl, combine baby spinach leaves, sliced strawberries, sliced almonds, and crumbled feta cheese.
2. In a small bowl, whisk together balsamic vinegar, extra virgin olive oil, honey, salt, and pepper to make the dressing.
3. Drizzle dressing over the salad and toss gently to combine.
4. Serve the Spinach and Strawberry Salad immediately.

Nutritional Information per serving:
Cal: 180 | Fat: 13g | Chol: 5mg | Sodium: 170mg | Carbs: 15g | Fiber: 4g | Sugars: 9g | Protein: 4g

KALE AND APPLE SALAD WITH LEMON VINAIGRETTE

Yield: 4 servings | Prep time: 15 minutes | Cook time: 0 minutes

Ingredients:

- 4 cups chopped kale leaves
- 1 apple, thinly sliced
- 1/4 cup dried cranberries
- 1/4 cup chopped walnuts
- 1/4 cup grated Parmesan cheese
- 2 tablespoons lemon juice
- 2 tablespoons extra virgin olive oil
- 1 teaspoon honey
- Salt and pepper to taste

Directions:

1. In a large bowl, combine chopped kale leaves, sliced apple, dried cranberries, chopped walnuts, and grated Parmesan cheese.
2. In a small bowl, whisk together lemon juice, extra virgin olive oil, honey, salt, and pepper to make the dressing.
3. Drizzle dressing over the salad and toss gently to combine.
4. Serve the Kale and Apple Salad immediately.

Nutritional Information per serving:

Cal: 250 | Fat: 16g | Chol: 5mg | Sodium: 160mg | Carbs: 24g | Fiber: 4g | Sugars: 14g | Protein: 6g

BEET AND GOAT CHEESE SALAD

Yield: 4 servings | Prep time: 15 minutes | Cook time: 0 minutes

Ingredients:

- 4 cups mixed salad greens
- 2 medium beets, cooked, peeled, and thinly sliced
- 1/4 cup crumbled goat cheese
- 2 tablespoons balsamic vinegar
- 2 tablespoons extra virgin olive oil
- 1 teaspoon Dijon mustard
- Salt and pepper to taste

Directions:

1. In a large bowl, arrange mixed salad greens. Top with sliced beets and crumbled goat cheese.
2. In a small bowl, whisk together balsamic vinegar, extra virgin olive oil, Dijon mustard, salt, and pepper to make the dressing.
3. Drizzle dressing over the salad and toss gently to combine.
4. Serve the Beet and Goat Cheese Salad immediately.

Nutritional Information per serving:

Cal: 190 | Fat: 14g | Chol: 5mg | Sodium: 160mg | Carbs: 12g | Fiber: 3g | Sugars: 8g | Protein: 5g

COBB SALAD WITH GRILLED CHICKEN

Yield: 4 servings | Prep time: 20 minutes | Cook time: 15 minutes

Ingredients:
- 4 cups mixed salad greens
- 2 grilled chicken breasts, sliced
- 4 hard-boiled eggs, sliced
- 6 slices cooked bacon, crumbled
- 1 avocado, diced
- 1 cup cherry tomatoes, halved
- 1/2 cup crumbled blue cheese
- 2 tablespoons red wine vinegar
- 2 tablespoons extra virgin olive oil
- 1 teaspoon Dijon mustard
- Salt and pepper to taste

Directions:
1. In a large bowl, arrange mixed salad greens. Top with sliced grilled chicken breasts, sliced hard-boiled eggs, crumbled bacon, diced avocado, cherry tomatoes, and crumbled blue cheese.
2. In a small bowl, whisk together red wine vinegar, extra virgin olive oil, Dijon mustard, salt, and pepper to make the dressing.
3. Drizzle dressing over the salad and toss gently to combine.
4. Serve the Cobb Salad with Grilled Chicken immediately.

Nutritional Information per serving:
Cal: 430 | Fat: 30g | Chol: 235mg | Sodium: 670mg | Carbs: 11g | Fiber: 5g | Sugars: 3g | Protein: 30g

ASIAN CUCUMBER SALAD

Yield: 4 servings | Prep time: 10 minutes | Cook time: 0 minutes

Ingredients:
- 2 cucumbers, thinly sliced
- 1/4 cup rice vinegar
- 1 tablespoon soy sauce
- 1 teaspoon sesame oil
- 1 teaspoon honey
- 1 tablespoon toasted sesame seeds
- 2 green onions, thinly sliced
- Salt and pepper to taste

Directions:
1. In a large bowl, combine thinly sliced cucumbers and sliced green onions.
2. In a small bowl, whisk together rice vinegar, soy sauce, sesame oil, honey, salt, and pepper to make the dressing.
3. Drizzle dressing over the cucumber mixture and toss gently to combine.
4. Sprinkle toasted sesame seeds over the salad.
5. Serve the Asian Cucumber Salad immediately.

Nutritional Information per serving:
Cal: 45 | Fat: 2g | Chol: 0mg | Sodium: 210mg | Carbs: 7g | Fiber: 1g | Sugars: 4g | Protein: 1g

WALDORF SALAD WITH YOGURT DRESSING

Yield: 4 servings | Prep time: 15 minutes | Cook time: 0 minutes

Ingredients:
- 2 apples, diced
- 1 cup diced celery
- 1/2 cup halved grapes
- 1/4 cup chopped walnuts
- 1/4 cup plain Greek yogurt
- 1 tablespoon lemon juice
- 1 tablespoon honey
- Salt and pepper to taste
- Mixed salad greens for serving

Directions:
1. In a large bowl, combine diced apples, diced celery, halved grapes, and chopped walnuts.
2. In a small bowl, whisk together plain Greek yogurt, lemon juice, honey, salt, and pepper to make the dressing.
3. Drizzle dressing over the fruit and nut mixture and toss gently to combine.
4. Serve the Waldorf Salad over mixed salad greens.

Nutritional Information per serving:
Cal: 160 | Fat: 7g | Chol: 0mg | Sodium: 40mg | Carbs: 25g | Fiber: 4g | Sugars: 18g | Protein: 4g

ARUGULA AND PEAR SALAD WITH WALNUTS

Yield: 4 servings | Prep time: 10 minutes | Cook time: 0 minutes

Ingredients:
- 4 cups arugula leaves
- 2 ripe pears, thinly sliced
- 1/4 cup chopped walnuts
- 1/4 cup crumbled feta cheese
- 2 tablespoons balsamic vinegar
- 2 tablespoons extra virgin olive oil
- Salt and pepper to taste

Directions:
1. In a large bowl, combine arugula leaves, thinly sliced pears, chopped walnuts, and crumbled feta cheese.
2. In a small bowl, whisk together balsamic vinegar, extra virgin olive oil, salt, and pepper to make the dressing.
3. Drizzle dressing over the salad and toss gently to combine.
4. Serve the Arugula and Pear Salad immediately.

Nutritional Information per serving:
Cal: 200 | Fat: 14g | Chol: 0mg | Sodium: 160mg | Carbs: 18g | Fiber: 4g | Sugars: 12g | Protein: 4g

WATERMELON AND FETA SALAD WITH MINT

Yield: 4 servings | Prep time: 10 minutes | Cook time: 0 minutes

Ingredients:
- 4 cups cubed watermelon
- 1/2 cup crumbled feta cheese
- 1/4 cup chopped fresh mint leaves
- 2 tablespoons balsamic vinegar
- 1 tablespoon extra virgin olive oil
- Salt and pepper to taste

Directions:
1. In a large bowl, combine cubed watermelon, crumbled feta cheese, and chopped fresh mint leaves.
2. In a small bowl, whisk together balsamic vinegar, extra virgin olive oil, salt, and pepper to make the dressing.
3. Drizzle dressing over the salad and toss gently to combine.
4. Serve the Watermelon and Feta Salad immediately.

Nutritional Information per serving:
Cal: 120 | Fat: 6g | Chol: 15mg | Sodium: 240mg | Carbs: 15g | Fiber: 1g | Sugars: 12g | Protein: 3g

ORANGE AND FENNEL SALAD

Yield: 4 servings | Prep time: 15 minutes | Cook time: 0 minutes

Ingredients:
- 2 oranges, peeled and sliced
- 1 fennel bulb, thinly sliced
- 1/4 cup chopped fresh parsley
- 1/4 cup chopped walnuts
- 2 tablespoons orange juice
- 2 tablespoons extra virgin olive oil
- 1 teaspoon honey
- Salt and pepper to taste

Directions:
1. In a large bowl, combine sliced oranges, thinly sliced fennel bulb, chopped fresh parsley, and chopped walnuts.
2. In a small bowl, whisk together orange juice, extra virgin olive oil, honey, salt, and pepper to make the dressing.
3. Drizzle dressing over the salad and toss gently to combine.
4. Serve the Orange and Fennel Salad immediately.

Nutritional Information per serving:
Cal: 150 | Fat: 11g | Chol: 0mg | Sodium: 10mg | Carbs: 14g | Fiber: 4g | Sugars: 9g | Protein: 2g

GREEK YOGURT DIP WITH VEGETABLES

Yield: 4 servings | Prep time: 10 minutes | Cook time: 0 minutes

Ingredients:
- 1 cup plain Greek yogurt
- 1 tablespoon lemon juice
- 1 clove garlic, minced
- 1 tablespoon chopped fresh dill
- Salt and pepper to taste
- Assorted vegetables for dipping (carrot sticks, cucumber slices, bell pepper strips, cherry tomatoes, etc.)

Directions:
1. In a small bowl, mix together Greek yogurt, lemon juice, minced garlic, chopped fresh dill, salt, and pepper until well combined.
2. Serve the Greek yogurt dip with assorted vegetables for dipping.

Nutritional Information per serving:
Cal: 45 | Fat: 0g | Chol: 0mg | Sodium: 30mg | Carbs: 3g | Fiber: 0g | Sugars: 2g | Protein: 8g

HUMMUS AND WHOLE WHEAT PITA CHIPS

Yield: 4 servings | Prep time: 10 minutes | Cook time: 10 minutes

Ingredients:
- 1 can (15 ounces) chickpeas, drained and rinsed
- 2 tablespoons tahini
- 2 tablespoons lemon juice
- 1 clove garlic, minced
- 2 tablespoons extra virgin olive oil
- Salt and pepper to taste
- 2 whole wheat pita breads, cut into wedges

Directions:
1. In a food processor, combine chickpeas, tahini, lemon juice, minced garlic, extra virgin olive oil, salt, and pepper. Blend until smooth.
2. Preheat oven to 375°F (190°C).
3. Place whole wheat pita wedges on a baking sheet. Bake for 8-10 minutes, or until crisp.
4. Serve the hummus with whole wheat pita chips.

Nutritional Information per serving:
Cal: 180 | Fat: 8g | Chol: 0mg | Sodium: 170mg | Carbs: 22g | Fiber: 4g | Sugars: 1g | Protein: 6g

COTTAGE CHEESE WITH PINEAPPLE CHUNKS

Yield: 4 servings | Prep time: 5 minutes | Cook time: 0 minutes

Ingredients:
- 1 cup low-fat cottage cheese
- 1 cup pineapple chunks (fresh or canned in juice, drained)

Directions:
1. Divide low-fat cottage cheese into individual serving bowls.
2. Top each serving with pineapple chunks.
3. Serve the Cottage Cheese with Pineapple Chunks chilled.

Nutritional Information per serving:
Cal: 110 | Fat: 1g | Chol: 5mg | Sodium: 380mg | Carbs: 13g | Fiber: 1g | Sugars: 10g | Protein: 14g

WHOLE GRAIN CRACKERS WITH TZATZIKI

Yield: 4 servings | Prep time: 10 minutes | Cook time: 0 minutes

Ingredients:
- 1 cup plain Greek yogurt
- 1/2 cucumber, grated and squeezed to remove excess moisture
- 1 clove garlic, minced
- 1 tablespoon chopped fresh dill
- 1 tablespoon lemon juice
- Salt and pepper to taste
- Whole grain crackers for serving

Directions:
1. In a medium bowl, combine Greek yogurt, grated cucumber, minced garlic, chopped fresh dill, lemon juice, salt, and pepper to make the tzatziki.
2. Chill the tzatziki in the refrigerator for at least 30 minutes.
3. Serve the tzatziki with whole grain crackers.

Nutritional Information per serving:
Cal: 80 | Fat: 3g | Chol: 5mg | Sodium: 90mg | Carbs: 6g | Fiber: 1g | Sugars: 2g | Protein: 7g

DEVILED EGGS WITH AVOCADO

Yield: 4 servings | Prep time: 15 minutes | Cook time: 10 minutes

Ingredients:
- 4 hard-boiled eggs, peeled and halved
- 1 ripe avocado
- 1 tablespoon Greek yogurt
- 1 teaspoon Dijon mustard
- 1 teaspoon lemon juice
- Salt and pepper to taste
- Paprika for garnish

Directions:
1. Remove egg yolks from hard-boiled eggs and place them in a bowl. Mash egg yolks with avocado, Greek yogurt, Dijon mustard, lemon juice, salt, and pepper until smooth.
2. Spoon avocado mixture back into the egg white halves.
3. Sprinkle deviled eggs with paprika.
4. Serve the Deviled Eggs with Avocado chilled.

Nutritional Information per serving:
Cal: 110 | Fat: 8g | Chol: 185mg | Sodium: 85mg | Carbs: 3g | Fiber: 2g | Sugars: 0g | Protein: 6g

SPICY EDAMAME

Yield: 4 servings | Prep time: 10 minutes | Cook time: 5 minutes

Ingredients:
- 2 cups frozen edamame (unshelled)
- 1 tablespoon sesame oil
- 1 teaspoon soy sauce
- 1/2 teaspoon sriracha sauce (adjust to taste)
- Sesame seeds for garnish (optional)

Directions:
1. Cook frozen edamame according to package instructions. Drain and set aside.
2. In a skillet, heat sesame oil over medium heat. Add cooked edamame, soy sauce, and sriracha sauce. Stir-fry for 2-3 minutes.
3. Sprinkle spicy edamame with sesame seeds, if desired.
4. Serve the Spicy Edamame hot or at room temperature.

Nutritional Information per serving:
Cal: 110 | Fat: 6g | Chol: 0mg | Sodium: 55mg | Carbs: 8g | Fiber: 4g | Sugars: 2g | Protein: 9g

SMOKED SALMON CUCUMBER BITES

Yield: 4 servings | Prep time: 10 minutes | Cook time: 0 minutes

Ingredients:

- 1 cucumber, sliced into rounds
- 4 ounces smoked salmon
- 2 tablespoons Greek yogurt
- 1 tablespoon chopped fresh dill
- 1 teaspoon lemon juice
- Salt and pepper to taste

Directions:

1. Place cucumber rounds on a serving platter.
2. Top each cucumber round with a small piece of smoked salmon.
3. In a small bowl, mix together Greek yogurt, chopped fresh dill, lemon juice, salt, and pepper.
4. Spoon a small amount of the yogurt mixture onto each cucumber and smoked salmon bite.
5. Serve the Smoked Salmon Cucumber Bites chilled.

Nutritional Information per serving:

Cal: 70 | Fat: 3g | Chol: 10mg | Sodium: 150mg | Carbs: 2g | Fiber: 0g | Sugars: 1g | Protein: 8g

BAKED SWEET POTATO FRIES

Yield: 4 servings | Prep time: 10 minutes | Cook time: 25 minutes

Ingredients:

- 2 large sweet potatoes, cut into fries
- 1 tablespoon olive oil
- 1 teaspoon smoked paprika
- 1/2 teaspoon garlic powder
- Salt and pepper to taste

Directions:

1. Preheat oven to 425°F (220°C). Line a baking sheet with parchment paper.
2. In a large bowl, toss sweet potato fries with olive oil, smoked paprika, garlic powder, salt, and pepper until evenly coated.
3. Spread sweet potato fries in a single layer on the prepared baking sheet.
4. Bake for 20-25 minutes, flipping halfway through, until fries are golden and crispy.
5. Serve the Baked Sweet Potato Fries hot.

Nutritional Information per serving:

Cal: 140 | Fat: 3.5g | Chol: 0mg | Sodium: 90mg | Carbs: 25g | Fiber: 4g | Sugars: 6g | Protein: 2g

ANTIPASTO SKEWERS WITH OLIVES AND CHERRY TOMATOES

Yield: 4 servings | Prep time: 15 minutes | Cook time: 0 minutes

Ingredients:
- 16 pitted Kalamata olives
- 16 cherry tomatoes
- 16 small mozzarella balls (bocconcini)
- 16 slices of salami or prosciutto
- 16 fresh basil leaves
- Balsamic glaze for drizzling (optional)
- Wooden skewers

Directions:
1. Thread olives, cherry tomatoes, mozzarella balls, salami slices, and fresh basil leaves onto wooden skewers, alternating ingredients.
2. Arrange skewers on a serving platter.
3. Drizzle with balsamic glaze, if desired.
4. Serve the Antipasto Skewers immediately.

Nutritional Information per serving:
Cal: 180 | Fat: 12g | Chol: 30mg | Sodium: 460mg | Carbs: 4g | Fiber: 1g | Sugars: 2g | Protein: 11g

ALMOND AND DATE ENERGY BALLS

Yield: 12 servings (2 balls per serving) | Prep time: 15 minutes | Cook time: 0 minutes

Ingredients:
- 1 cup pitted dates
- 1 cup almonds
- 2 tablespoons unsweetened cocoa powder
- 1 tablespoon honey
- 1/2 teaspoon vanilla extract
- Pinch of salt
- Shredded coconut or cocoa powder for coating (optional)

Directions:
1. Place dates, almonds, cocoa powder, honey, vanilla extract, and salt in a food processor. Pulse until mixture comes together and forms a sticky dough.
2. Roll mixture into small balls, about 1 tablespoon each.
3. If desired, roll energy balls in shredded coconut or cocoa powder to coat.
4. Chill energy balls in the refrigerator for at least 30 minutes before serving.
5. Serve the Almond and Date Energy Balls chilled.

Nutritional Information per serving:
Cal: 150 | Fat: 8g | Chol: 0mg | Sodium: 0mg | Carbs: 19g | Fiber: 3g | Sugars: 14g | Protein: 3g

Chapter 10
DESSERTS AND TREATS

AVOCADO CHOCOLATE MOUSSE

Yield: 4 servings | Prep time: 10 minutes | Cook time: 0 minutes

Ingredients:

- 2 ripe avocados
- 1/4 cup cocoa powder
- 1/4 cup maple syrup or honey
- 1 teaspoon vanilla extract
- Pinch of salt
- Optional toppings: fresh berries, shaved chocolate, chopped nuts

Directions:

1. Cut the avocados in half, remove the pits, and scoop the flesh into a blender or food processor.
2. Add cocoa powder, maple syrup or honey, vanilla extract, and a pinch of salt to the blender.
3. Blend until the mixture is smooth and creamy, scraping down the sides of the blender as needed.
4. Taste and adjust sweetness if necessary by adding more maple syrup or honey.
5. Divide the avocado chocolate mousse into serving dishes.
6. Chill in the refrigerator for at least 30 minutes before serving.
7. Garnish with fresh berries, shaved chocolate, or chopped nuts before serving, if desired.

Nutritional Information per serving:

Cal: 170 | Fat: 10g | Chol: 0mg | Sodium: 10mg | Carbs: 20g | Fiber: 7g | Sugars: 10g | Protein: 3g

BANANA OATMEAL COOKIES

Yield: 12 cookies | Prep time: 10 minutes | Cook time: 15 minutes

Ingredients:

- 2 ripe bananas, mashed
- 1 cup rolled oats
- 1/4 cup almond flour
- 1/4 cup chopped walnuts or almonds
- 1/4 cup raisins or dried cranberries (optional)
- 1 teaspoon cinnamon
- Pinch of salt

Directions:

1. Preheat the oven to 350°F (175°C). Line a baking sheet with parchment paper.
2. In a mixing bowl, combine mashed bananas, rolled oats, almond flour, chopped nuts, raisins or dried cranberries (if using), cinnamon, and salt. Stir until well combined.
3. Drop spoonfuls of the cookie dough onto the prepared baking sheet, and flatten each cookie slightly with the back of a spoon.
4. Bake for 15-18 minutes, or until the cookies are golden brown and set.
5. Allow the cookies to cool on the baking sheet for 5 minutes before transferring them to a wire rack to cool completely.

Nutritional Information per serving:

Cal: 90 | Fat: 3.5g | Chol: 0mg | Sodium: 0mg | Carbs: 14g | Fiber: 2g | Sugars: 4g | Protein: 2g

LEMON BLUEBERRY MUFFINS WITH WHOLE WHEAT FLOUR

Yield: 12 muffins | Prep time: 15 minutes | Cook time: 20 minutes

MANGO COCONUT POPSICLES

Yield: 6 popsicles | Prep time: 10 minutes | Freeze time: 4 hours

Ingredients:

- 2 ripe mangoes, peeled and diced
- 1 cup coconut milk
- 2 tablespoons honey or maple syrup
- 1/2 teaspoon vanilla extract
- Shredded coconut for coating (optional)

Directions:

1. Place diced mangoes, coconut milk, honey or maple syrup, and vanilla extract in a blender. Blend until smooth and creamy.
2. Pour the mango mixture into popsicle molds, filling each mold to the top.
3. If desired, sprinkle shredded coconut over the top of each popsicle.
4. Insert popsicle sticks into each mold and freeze for at least 4 hours, or until the popsicles are completely frozen.
5. To remove the popsicles from the molds, run warm water over the outside of the molds for a few seconds until the popsicles loosen.

Nutritional Information per serving:

Cal: 120 | Fat: 6g | Chol: 0mg | Sodium: 0mg | Carbs: 17g | Fiber: 1g | Sugars: 14g | Protein: 1g

Ingredients:

- 1 1/2 cups whole wheat flour
- 1/2 cup rolled oats
- 1/2 cup coconut sugar or brown sugar
- 2 teaspoons baking powder
- 1/2 teaspoon baking soda
- 1/4 teaspoon salt
- 1 cup unsweetened almond milk (or any milk of your choice)
- 1/4 cup melted coconut oil or unsweetened applesauce
- 1/4 cup fresh lemon juice
- 1 tablespoon lemon zest
- 1 teaspoon vanilla extract
- 1 cup fresh or frozen blueberries

Directions:

1. Preheat the oven to 375°F (190°C). Line a muffin tin with paper liners or grease with cooking spray.
2. In a large mixing bowl, combine whole wheat flour, rolled oats, coconut sugar or brown sugar, baking powder, baking soda, and salt.
3. In a separate bowl, whisk together almond milk, melted coconut oil or unsweetened applesauce, lemon juice, lemon zest, and vanilla extract.
4. Pour the wet ingredients into the dry ingredients and stir until just combined.
5. Gently fold in the blueberries.
6. Divide the batter evenly among the prepared muffin cups, filling each cup about 2/3 full.
7. Bake for 18-20 minutes, or until a toothpick inserted into the muffin comes out clean.
8. Allow the muffins to cool in the pan for 5 minutes before transferring them to a wire rack.

Nutritional Information per serving:

Cal: 160 | Fat: 5g | Chol: 0mg | Sodium: 140mg | Carbs: 26g | Fiber: 3g | Sugars: 9g | Protein: 3g

ALMOND FLOUR CHOCOLATE CHIP COOKIES

Yield: 12 cookies | Prep time: 10 minutes | Cook time: 12 minutes

Ingredients:

- 1 1/2 cups almond flour
- 1/4 teaspoon baking soda
- Pinch of salt
- 1/4 cup coconut oil, melted
- 1/4 cup honey or maple syrup
- 1 teaspoon vanilla extract
- 1/4 cup dark chocolate chips

Directions:

1. Preheat the oven to 350°F (175°C). Line a baking sheet with parchment paper.
2. In a mixing bowl, whisk together almond flour, baking soda, and salt.
3. Stir in melted coconut oil, honey or maple syrup, and vanilla extract until well combined.
4. Fold in dark chocolate chips.
5. Drop spoonfuls of dough onto the prepared baking sheet, and flatten each cookie slightly with the back of a spoon.
6. Bake for 10-12 minutes, or until the cookies are golden brown around the edges.
7. Allow the cookies to cool on the baking sheet for 5 minutes before transferring them to a wire rack to cool completely.

Nutritional Information per serving:

Cal: 140 | Fat: 10g | Chol: 0mg | Sodium: 40mg | Carbs: 10g | Fiber: 2g | Sugars: 7g | Protein: 3g

APPLE CINNAMON QUINOA BREAKFAST BARS

Yield: 12 bars | Prep time: 15 minutes | Cook time: 30 minutes

Ingredients:

- 1 cup cooked quinoa
- 1 cup rolled oats
- 1/2 cup unsweetened applesauce
- 1/4 cup honey or maple syrup
- 1 teaspoon cinnamon
- 1/2 teaspoon vanilla extract
- 1/4 teaspoon salt
- 1/2 cup diced apples
- 1/4 cup chopped walnuts or almonds (optional)

Directions:

1. Preheat the oven to 350°F (175°C). Grease or line a baking dish with parchment paper.
2. In a large mixing bowl, combine cooked quinoa, rolled oats, applesauce, honey or maple syrup, cinnamon, vanilla extract, and salt. Stir until well combined.
3. Fold in diced apples and chopped nuts, if using.
4. Transfer the mixture to the prepared baking dish and spread it out evenly.
5. Bake for 25-30 minutes, or until the edges are golden brown and the bars are set.
6. Allow the bars to cool completely before slicing into squares or bars.

Nutritional Information per serving:

Cal: 110 | Fat: 2g | Chol: 0mg | Sodium: 50mg | Carbs: 22g | Fiber: 2g | Sugars: 9g | Protein: 2g

STRAWBERRY BANANA NICE CREAM

Yield: 2 servings | Prep time: 5 minutes | Freeze time: 4 hours

Ingredients:
- 2 ripe bananas, sliced and frozen
- 1 cup frozen strawberries
- 1/4 cup unsweetened almond milk (or any milk of your choice)
- 1 teaspoon vanilla extract

Directions:
1. Place frozen banana slices, frozen strawberries, almond milk, and vanilla extract in a blender or food processor.
2. Blend until smooth and creamy, scraping down the sides of the blender or food processor as needed.
3. If the nice cream is too thick, add more almond milk, 1 tablespoon at a time, until desired consistency is reached.
4. Serve the strawberry banana nice cream immediately as a soft-serve dessert, or transfer it to a freezer-safe container and freeze for 1-2 hours for a firmer texture.

Nutritional Information per serving:
Cal: 140 | Fat: 1g | Chol: 0mg | Sodium: 0mg | Carbs: 34g | Fiber: 5g | Sugars: 19g | Protein: 2g

PUMPKIN SPICE ENERGY BALLS

Yield: 12 balls | Prep time: 10 minutes | Cook time: 0 minutes

Ingredients:
- 1 cup rolled oats
- 1/2 cup canned pumpkin puree
- 1/4 cup almond butter or peanut butter
- 2 tablespoons honey or maple syrup
- 1 teaspoon pumpkin pie spice
- Pinch of salt
- Optional add-ins: chopped nuts, dried cranberries, chocolate chips

Directions:
1. In a mixing bowl, combine rolled oats, pumpkin puree, almond butter or peanut butter, honey or maple syrup, pumpkin pie spice, and salt. Stir until well combined.
2. If desired, fold in chopped nuts, dried cranberries, or chocolate chips.
3. Roll the mixture into balls, using about 1 tablespoon of mixture for each ball.
4. Place the energy balls on a baking sheet lined with parchment paper.
5. Chill the energy balls in the refrigerator for at least 30 minutes before serving.

Nutritional Information per serving:
Cal: 90 | Fat: 4g | Chol: 0mg | Sodium: 20mg | Carbs: 12g | Fiber: 2g | Sugars: 4g | Protein: 2g

ORANGE CRANBERRY OATMEAL COOKIES

Yield: 12 cookies | Prep time: 10 minutes | Cook time: 12 minutes

Ingredients:
- 1 cup rolled oats
- 1/2 cup whole wheat flour
- 1/4 cup coconut sugar or brown sugar
- 1/2 teaspoon baking powder
- 1/4 teaspoon baking soda
- Pinch of salt
- 1/4 cup unsweetened applesauce
- 2 tablespoons coconut oil, melted
- 1 tablespoon orange zest
- 2 tablespoons fresh orange juice
- 1/4 cup dried cranberries

Directions:
1. Preheat the oven to 350°F (175°C). Line a baking sheet with parchment paper.
2. In a mixing bowl, combine rolled oats, whole wheat flour, coconut sugar or brown sugar, baking powder, baking soda, and salt.
3. In a separate bowl, whisk together applesauce, melted coconut oil, orange zest, and orange juice.
4. Pour the wet ingredients into the dry ingredients and stir until well combined.
5. Fold in dried cranberries.
6. Drop spoonfuls of dough onto the prepared baking sheet, and flatten each cookie slightly with the back of a spoon.
7. Bake for 10-12 minutes, or until the cookies are golden brown around the edges.
8. Allow the cookies to cool on the baking sheet for 5 minutes before transferring them to a wire rack to cool completely.

Nutritional Information per serving:
Cal: 100 | Fat: 3g | Chol: 0mg | Sodium: 45mg | Carbs: 17g | Fiber: 2g | Sugars: 6g | Protein: 2g

COCONUT FLOUR PANCAKES WITH FRESH FRUIT

Yield: 6 pancakes | Prep time: 10 minutes | Cook time: 10 minutes

Ingredients:
- 1/2 cup coconut flour
- 1 teaspoon baking powder
- Pinch of salt
- 4 large eggs
- 1/2 cup unsweetened almond milk (or any milk of your choice)
- 2 tablespoons honey or maple syrup
- 1 teaspoon vanilla extract
- Fresh fruit for serving

Directions:
1. In a mixing bowl, whisk together coconut flour, baking powder, and salt.
2. In a separate bowl, beat eggs, almond milk, honey or maple syrup, and vanilla extract until well combined.
3. Pour the wet ingredients into the dry ingredients and whisk until smooth.
4. Heat a non-stick skillet or griddle over medium heat. Lightly grease with cooking spray or coconut oil.
5. Pour 1/4 cup of batter onto the skillet for each pancake. Cook until bubbles form on the surface, then flip and cook until golden brown on the other side.
6. Repeat with the remaining batter.
7. Serve the coconut flour pancakes topped with fresh fruit.

Nutritional Information per serving:
Cal: 90 | Fat: 4g | Chol: 95mg | Sodium: 90mg | Carbs: 8g | Fiber: 3g | Sugars: 5g | Protein: 5g

Chapter 11
BEVERAGES & TEAS

GREEN SMOOTHIE WITH SPINACH AND BANANA

LEMON GINGER TEA

Yield: 2 servings | Prep time: 5 minutes | Cook time: 0 minutes

Yield: 1 serving | Prep time: 5 minutes | Cook time: 5 minutes

Ingredients:
- 2 cups fresh spinach leaves
- 1 ripe banana
- 1 cup almond milk (unsweetened)
- 1/2 cup plain Greek yogurt
- 1 tablespoon honey or maple syrup (optional)
- Ice cubes (optional)

Directions:
1. Place all ingredients in a blender.
2. Blend until smooth.
3. If desired, add ice cubes and blend again until smooth.
4. Serve immediately.

Nutritional Information per serving:
Cal: 110 | Fat: 2g | Chol: 0mg | Sodium: 140mg | Carbs: 20g | Fiber: 3g | Sugars: 12g | Protein: 6g

Ingredients:
- 1-inch piece of fresh ginger, thinly sliced
- 2 cups water
- Juice of 1 lemon
- Honey or maple syrup to taste (optional)
- Lemon slices for garnish (optional)

Directions:
1. In a small saucepan, combine ginger slices and water.
2. Bring to a boil, then reduce heat and simmer for 10 minutes.
3. Remove from heat and stir in lemon juice.
4. Strain the tea into a mug and sweeten with honey or maple syrup if desired.
5. Garnish with lemon slices if desired.
6. Serve hot.

Nutritional Information per serving:
Cal: 10 | Fat: 0g | Chol: 0mg | Sodium: 5mg | Carbs: 3g | Fiber: 0g | Sugars: 0g | Protein: 0g

BERRY BLAST SMOOTHIE

Yield: 2 servings | Prep time: 5 minutes | Cook time: 0 minutes

Ingredients:

- 1 cup mixed berries (strawberries, blueberries, raspberries)
- 1/2 cup plain Greek yogurt
- 1/2 cup almond milk (unsweetened)
- 1 tablespoon honey or maple syrup (optional)
- Ice cubes (optional)

Directions:

1. Combine all ingredients in a blender.
2. Blend until smooth.
3. Add ice cubes if desired and blend again until smooth.
4. Serve immediately.

Nutritional Information per serving:

Cal: 110 | Fat: 2g | Chol: 0mg | Sodium: 45mg | Carbs: 20g | Fiber: 5g | Sugars: 12g | Protein: 6g

GOLDEN TURMERIC LATTE

Yield: 1 serving | Prep time: 5 minutes | Cook time: 5 minutes

Ingredients:

- 1 cup unsweetened almond milk
- 1 teaspoon ground turmeric
- 1/2 teaspoon ground cinnamon
- Pinch of ground black pepper
- 1 teaspoon honey or maple syrup (optional)

Directions:

1. In a small saucepan, heat almond milk over medium heat until warmed but not boiling.
2. Whisk in turmeric, cinnamon, black pepper, and honey or maple syrup (if using).
3. Continue to whisk until ingredients are well combined and the mixture is heated through.
4. Pour into a mug and serve hot.

Nutritional Information per serving:

Cal: 60 | Fat: 2g | Chol: 0mg | Sodium: 160mg | Carbs: 10g | Fiber: 2g | Sugars: 6g | Protein: 2g

STRAWBERRY BASIL LEMONADE

Yield: 2 servings | Prep time: 5 minutes | Cook time: 0 minutes

Ingredients:

- 1 cup fresh strawberries, hulled
- 4-5 fresh basil leaves
- Juice of 2 lemons
- 2 cups cold water
- 1-2 tablespoons honey or maple syrup (optional)
- Ice cubes
- Lemon slices and basil leaves for garnish (optional)

Directions:

1. In a blender, combine strawberries, basil leaves, lemon juice, water, and honey or maple syrup (if using).
2. Blend until smooth.
3. Strain the mixture through a fine mesh sieve to remove seeds and pulp (if desired).
4. Serve over ice cubes, garnished with lemon slices and basil leaves if desired.

Nutritional Information per serving:

Cal: 50 | Fat: 0g | Chol: 0mg | Sodium: 10mg | Carbs: 14g | Fiber: 2g | Sugars: 8g | Protein: 1g

HIBISCUS GREEN TEA

Yield: 2 servings | Prep time: 5 minutes | Cook time: 5 minutes

Ingredients:

- 2 hibiscus tea bags
- 2 green tea bags
- 4 cups hot water
- Honey or maple syrup to taste (optional)
- Lemon slices for garnish (optional)

Directions:

1. Place hibiscus tea bags and green tea bags in a teapot or pitcher.
2. Pour hot water over the tea bags.
3. Steep for 3-5 minutes.
4. Remove tea bags and sweeten with honey or maple syrup if desired.
5. Garnish with lemon slices if desired.
6. Serve hot.

Nutritional Information per serving:

Cal: 0 | Fat: 0g | Chol: 0mg | Sodium: 0mg | Carbs: 0g | Fiber: 0g | Sugars: 0g | Protein: 0g

CARROT ORANGE GINGER JUICE

Yield: 2 servings | Prep time: 5 minutes | Cook time: 0 minutes

Ingredients:

- 4 large carrots, peeled and chopped
- 2 oranges, peeled and segmented
- 1-inch piece of fresh ginger, peeled
- 1 tablespoon honey or maple syrup (optional)
- Ice cubes (optional)

Directions:

1. Pass carrots, oranges, and ginger through a juicer.
2. Stir in honey or maple syrup if desired.
3. Serve over ice cubes if desired.

Nutritional Information per serving:

Cal: 90 | Fat: 0g | Chol: 0mg | Sodium: 60mg | Carbs: 22g | Fiber: 4g | Sugars: 15g | Protein: 2g

CRANBERRY POMEGRANATE SPARKLER

Yield: 2 servings | Prep time: 5 minutes | Cook time: 0 minutes

Ingredients:

- 1/2 cup cranberry juice (unsweetened)
- 1/2 cup pomegranate juice (unsweetened)
- 1 cup sparkling water or club soda
- Ice cubes
- Fresh mint leaves for garnish (optional)

Directions:

1. In a glass, combine cranberry juice and pomegranate juice.
2. Add sparkling water or club soda and stir gently to combine.
3. Add ice cubes and garnish with fresh mint leaves if desired.
4. Serve immediately.

Nutritional Information per serving:

Cal: 40 | Fat: 0g | Chol: 0mg | Sodium: 20mg | Carbs: 10g | Fiber: 0g | Sugars: 8g | Protein: 0g

GINGER TURMERIC TEA

Yield: 1 serving | Prep time: 5 minutes | Cook time: 5 minutes

Ingredients:

- 1-inch piece of fresh ginger, thinly sliced
- 1 teaspoon ground turmeric
- 2 cups water
- Honey or maple syrup to taste (optional)
- Lemon slices for garnish (optional)

Directions:

1. In a small saucepan, combine ginger slices and water.
2. Bring to a boil, then reduce heat and simmer for 10 minutes.
3. Strain the tea into a mug and sweeten with honey or maple syrup if desired.
4. Garnish with lemon slices if desired.
5. Serve hot.

Nutritional Information per serving:

Cal: 10 | Fat: 0g | Chol: 0mg | Sodium: 5mg | Carbs: 3g | Fiber: 1g | Sugars: 0g | Protein: 0g

CHAMOMILE LAVENDER TEA

Yield: 1 serving | Prep time: 5 minutes | Cook time: 5 minutes

Ingredients:

- 1 chamomile tea bag
- 1/2 teaspoon dried lavender buds
- 2 cups hot water
- Honey or maple syrup to taste (optional)
- Fresh lavender sprigs for garnish (optional)

Directions:

1. Place chamomile tea bag and dried lavender buds in a teapot or mug.
2. Pour hot water over the tea bag and lavender buds.
3. Steep for 5 minutes.
4. Remove tea bag and lavender buds.
5. Sweeten with honey or maple syrup if desired.
6. Garnish with fresh lavender sprigs if desired.
7. Serve hot.

Nutritional Information per serving:

Cal: 0 | Fat: 0g | Chol: 0mg | Sodium: 0mg | Carbs: 0g | Fiber: 0g | Sugars: 0g | Protein: 0g

Chapter 12
BONUSES AND USEFUL MATERIALS

30-DAY MEAL PLAN

Day	BREAKFAST	LUNCH	DINNER	SNACK
Day 1	Oatmeal with Fresh Fruit p.10	Turkey and Avocado Wrap p.16	Baked Garlic Parmesan Chicken p.34	Greek Yogurt Dip with Vegetables p.52
Day 2	Vegetable Omelette for DASH Diet p.10	Grilled Chicken and Vegetable Skewers p.16	Black Bean and Corn Quesadillas p.22	Hummus and Whole Wheat Pita Chips p.52
Day 3	Whole Grain Pancakes with Blueberry Compote p.11	Mediterranean Eggplant and Zucchini Bake p.17	Turkey Meatballs in Marinara Sauce p.25	Cottage Cheese with Pineapple Chunks p.53
Day 4	Avocado Toast with Poached Egg p.11	Salmon and Asparagus Foil Packets p.17	Vegetable and Lentil Curry p.26	Whole Grain Crackers with Tzatziki p.53
Day 5	Quinoa Breakfast Bowl p.12	Chicken and Brown Rice Stir-Fry p.18	Eggplant Parmesan p.26	Deviled Eggs with Avocado p.54
Day 6	Whole Wheat Breakfast Burrito p.12	Quinoa and Black Bean Stuffed Peppers p.18	Garlic Parmesan Crusted Salmon p.42	Spicy Edamame p.54
Day 7	Chia Seed Pudding with Mixed Berries p.13	Veggie and Lentil Soup p.19	Lemon Garlic Butter Scallops p.43	Smoked Salmon Cucumber Bites p.55
Day 8	Spinach and Feta Egg Muffins p.14	Ratatouille with Herbed Couscous p.23	Teriyaki Glazed Mahi Mahi p.41	Baked Sweet Potato Fries p.55
Day 9	Sweet Potato Hash with Turkey Sausage p.14	Quinoa and Black Bean Stuffed Peppers p.18	Mediterranean Stuffed Chicken Breasts p.35	Antipasto Skewers with Olives and Cherry Tomatoes p.56
Day 10	Oatmeal with Fresh Fruit p.10	Chicken and Vegetable Soup p.29	Baked Dijon Tilapia p.40	Almond and Date Energy Balls p.56

Day	BREAKFAST	LUNCH	DINNER	SNACK
Day 11	Avocado Toast with Poached Egg p.11	Spaghetti Squash with Marinara Sauce p.25	Pesto Turkey Meatballs p.37	Greek Yogurt Dip with Vegetables p.52
Day 12	Whole Grain Pancakes with Blueberry Compote p.11	Butternut Squash Soup p.30	Greek Style Grilled Lamb Chops p.37	Hummus and Whole Wheat Pita Chips p.52
Day 13	Quinoa Breakfast Bowl p.12	Balsamic Glazed Pork Chops p.36	Garlic Butter Lemon Shrimp Pasta p.44	Mango Coconut Popsicles p.59
Day 14	Chia Seed Pudding with Mixed Berries p.13	Vegetable Stir-Fry with Brown Rice p.19	Herb-Marinated Grilled Steak p.35	Smoked Salmon Cucumber Bites p.55
Day 15	Whole Wheat Breakfast Burrito p.12	Moroccan Chickpea Soup p.32	Mediterranean Baked Halibut p.42	Cottage Cheese with Pineapple Chunks p.53
Day 16	Spinach and Feta Egg Muffins p.14	Waldorf Salad with Yogurt Dressing p.49	Honey Mustard Glazed Chicken Thighs p.36	Whole Grain Crackers with Tzatziki p.53
Day 17	Avocado Toast with Poached Egg p.11	Vegetable and Lentil Curry p.26	Lemon Garlic Butter Scallops p.43	Apple Cinnamon Quinoa Breakfast Bars p.60
Day 18	Oatmeal with Fresh Fruit p.10	Asian Cucumber Salad p.48	Chicken and Brown Rice Stir-Fry p.18	Deviled Eggs with Avocado p.54
Day 19	Whole Grain Pancakes with Blueberry Compote p.11	Italian Wedding Soup p.28	Teriyaki Glazed Mahi Mahi p.41	Spicy Edamame p.54
Day 20	Quinoa Breakfast Bowl p.12	Greek Yogurt Dip with Vegetables p.52	Garlic Parmesan Crusted Salmon p.42	Almond Flour Chocolate Chip Cookies p.60

Day	BREAKFAST	LUNCH	DINNER	SNACK
Day 21	Chia Seed Pudding with Mixed Berries p.13	Quinoa and Black Bean Stuffed Peppers p.18	Vegetable Stir-Fry with Brown Rice p.19	Smoked Salmon Cucumber Bites p.55
Day 22	Whole Wheat Breakfast Burrito p.12	Tomato Basil Soup p.31	Baked Lemon Herb Trout p.44	Mango Coconut Popsicles p.59
Day 23	Vegetable Omelette for DASH Diet p.10	Beet and Goat Cheese Salad p.47	Spicy Sriracha Tuna Cakes p.40	Hummus and Whole Wheat Pita Chips p.52
Day 24	Whole Grain Pancakes with Blueberry Compote p.11	Cobb Salad with Grilled Chicken p.48	Herb-Marinated Grilled Steak p.35	Greek Yogurt Dip with Vegetables p.52
Day 25	Avocado Toast with Poached Egg p.11	Orange and Fennel Salad p.50	Pesto Turkey Meatballs p.37	Antipasto Skewers with Olives and Cherry Tomatoes p.56
Day 26	Quinoa Breakfast Bowl p.12	Asian Cucumber Salad p.48	Garlic Butter Lemon Shrimp Pasta p.44	Apple Cinnamon Quinoa Breakfast Bars p.60
Day 27	Chia Seed Pudding with Mixed Berries p.13	Mediterranean Eggplant and Zucchini Bake p.17	Honey Mustard Glazed Chicken Thighs p.36	Spicy Edamame p.54
Day 28	Oatmeal with Fresh Fruit p.10	Kale and Apple Salad with Lemon Vinaigrette p.47	Greek Style Grilled Lamb Chops p.37	Whole Grain Crackers with Tzatziki p.53
Day 29	Spinach and Feta Egg Muffins p.14	Spinach and White Bean Soup p.31	Lemon Garlic Butter Scallops p.43	Smoked Salmon Cucumber Bites p.55
Day 30	Whole Wheat Breakfast Burrito p.12	Tuna Nicoise Salad p.46	Baked Garlic Parmesan Chicken p.34	Almond and Date Energy Balls p.56

SHOPPING LISTS

Shopping List for 1-7 day Meal Plan

FRUITS & VEGETABLES
- Fresh fruits for oatmeal and snacks (e.g., berries, bananas)
- Avocado
- Vegetables for wraps, omelette, skewers, eggplant bake, asparagus packets, curry, stuffed peppers, soup, and snacks (e.g., lettuce, tomato, cucumber, bell peppers, zucchini, eggplant, asparagus, spinach)
- Fresh herbs for chicken skewers, eggplant bake, and salmon (e.g., parsley, basil, thyme)
- Blueberries for pancake compote
- Lemons for chicken skewers and salmon
- Garlic for chicken and garlic parmesan chicken
- Mixed berries for chia seed pudding

DAIRY & EGGS
- Greek yogurt for dip
- Eggs for omelette, poached eggs, and deviled eggs
- Cottage cheese for snack
- Parmesan cheese
- Butter

MEAT & SEAFOOD
- Turkey breast for wraps
- Chicken breast for skewers and stir-fry
- Salmon fillets for foil packets and salmon dish
- Ground turkey for meatballs
- Shrimp for snacks and shrimp dish

PANTRY
- Oatmeal
- Whole grain pancake mix
- Quinoa
- Black beans
- Corn tortillas for quesadillas
- Lentils
- Brown rice
- Whole wheat pita chips
- Hummus
- Crackers
- Chia seeds
- Canned tomatoes for sauce
- Bread crumbs for chicken dish

FROZEN
- Asparagus for foil packets
- Peas for stir-fry
- Edamame for snack

CONDIMENTS & SAUCES
- Olive oil
- Balsamic vinegar
- Soy sauce
- Teriyaki sauce
- Marinara sauce
- Tzatziki sauce
- Curry paste or powder

MISCELLANEOUS
- Skewers for grilling
- Aluminum foil for foil packets
- Toothpicks for deviled eggs

Shopping List for 8-14 day Meal Plan

FRUITS & VEGETABLES
- Fresh spinach and feta for egg muffins
- Fresh herbs for cooking (e.g., basil, oregano, thyme)
- Garlic for cooking
- Sweet potatoes for hash
- Bell peppers for stuffed peppers and stir-fry
- Eggplant, zucchini, tomatoes, onions, and other vegetables for ratatouille
- Blueberries for compote
- Sweet potatoes for fries
- Cherry tomatoes and olives for skewers
- Fresh fruit for oatmeal and snacks (e.g., berries)
- Avocado for toast and snack
- Lemons for cooking
- Spaghetti squash for lunch
- Butternut squash for soup
- Mangoes for popsicles

DAIRY & EGGS
- Feta cheese for egg muffins
- Eggs for muffins, poached eggs, and meatballs
- Parmesan cheese for pasta
- Greek yogurt for dip and breakfast
- Butter for cooking

MEAT & SEAFOOD
- Mahi Mahi fillets for dinner
- Turkey sausage for hash
- Ground turkey for meatballs
- Pork chops for dinner
- Lamb chops for dinner
- Shrimp for pasta
- Steak for dinner
- Smoked salmon for snack
- Tilapia fillets for dinner

PANTRY
- Oatmeal for breakfast
- Quinoa for breakfast and lunch
- Black beans for stuffed peppers
- Couscous for lunch
- Dijon mustard for tilapia
- Energy balls ingredients (e.g., almonds, dates)
- Pancake mix for breakfast
- Olive oil for cooking
- Balsamic vinegar for pork chops
- Whole wheat pasta for dinner
- Pita chips for snack
- Hummus for snack
- Coconut milk for popsicles
- Chia seeds for pudding

CONDIMENTS & SAUCES
- Teriyaki sauce for mahi mahi
- Marinara sauce for spaghetti squash
- Pesto sauce for meatballs
- Lemon butter sauce for shrimp
- Soy sauce for stir-fry
- Garlic butter for pasta

MISCELLANEOUS
- Skewers for grilling
- Toothpicks for snacks

Shopping List for 15-21 day Meal Plan

FRUITS & VEGETABLES
- Fresh spinach and feta for egg muffins
- Fresh herbs for cooking (e.g., parsley, cilantro)
- Garlic for cooking
- Avocado for toast and breakfast
- Lemons for cooking and salad dressing
- Pineapple for snack
- Apples for snack
- Fresh fruit for oatmeal and snacks (e.g., berries)
- Blueberries for compote and pancakes
- Cucumber for salad and snack
- Bell peppers for stir-fry and stuffed peppers
- Onions for cooking
- Carrots for curry and stir-fry
- Celery for soup
- Tomatoes for soup and salad
- Chickpeas for soup
- Lettuce for salad
- Asparagus for dinner
- Green onions for garnish
- Green beans for stir-fry
- Broccoli for stir-fry
- Snap peas for stir-fry

DAIRY & EGGS
- Feta cheese for egg muffins
- Eggs for muffins, poached eggs, and cooking
- Cottage cheese for snack
- Greek yogurt for dip and breakfast
- Butter for cooking
- Milk for pancakes and pudding
- Cheese for quesadillas

MEAT & SEAFOOD
- Scallops for dinner
- Halibut fillets for dinner
- Chicken thighs for dinner
- Mahi Mahi fillets for dinner
- Salmon fillets for dinner
- Shrimp for stir-fry
- Smoked salmon for snack

PANTRY
- Lentils for curry
- Whole wheat tortillas for burrito
- Quinoa for breakfast and lunch
- Black beans for burrito and soup
- Honey mustard for chicken
- Crackers for snack
- Rolled oats for breakfast
- Quinoa for bars
- Cinnamon for bars
- Pancake mix for breakfast
- Olive oil for cooking
- Rice for stir-fry
- Pasta for soup
- Chicken broth for soup
- Vegetable broth for soup
- Garlic powder for cooking
- Chocolate chips for cookies
- Almond flour for cookies

CONDIMENTS & SAUCES
- Tzatziki sauce for snack
- Lemon butter sauce for scallops
- Teriyaki sauce for fish
- Soy sauce for stir-fry
- Tomato sauce for soup

MISCELLANEOUS
- Skewers for grilling
- Toothpicks for snacks

Shopping List for 22-30 day Meal Plan

FRUITS & VEGETABLES
- Fresh vegetables for omelette, salad, and cooking (e.g., tomatoes, onions, bell peppers, spinach, zucchini, eggplant, fennel, kale, garlic)
- Fresh herbs for cooking and salad (e.g., basil, parsley, cilantro, dill)
- Avocado for toast, salad, and burrito
- Lemons for cooking, salad dressing, and lemonade
- Mango for popsicles
- Apples for salad and snack
- Blueberries for compote and pancakes
- Cucumber for salad and snack
- Beets for salad
- Cherry tomatoes for skewers and snack
- Olives for skewers
- Pineapple for snack
- Berries for oatmeal and snacks
- Oranges for salad and snack
- Potatoes for hash
- Shallots for cooking
- Green beans for salad and soup
- White beans for soup
- Scallions for soup
- Carrots for stir-fry and soup
- Cabbage for stir-fry

DAIRY & EGGS
- Eggs for omelette, poached eggs, and muffins
- Goat cheese for salad
- Greek yogurt for dip and breakfast
- Butter for cooking
- Parmesan cheese for chicken
- Feta cheese for muffins

MEAT & SEAFOOD
- Trout fillets for dinner
- Tuna for tuna cakes
- Chicken breasts for salad and dinner
- Steak for dinner
- Ground turkey for meatballs
- Shrimp for pasta
- Scallops for dinner
- Lamb chops for dinner
- Salmon for bites

PANTRY
- Whole wheat tortillas for burrito
- Quinoa for breakfast and lunch
- Rolled oats for breakfast
- Pancake mix for breakfast
- Olive oil for cooking
- Honey mustard for chicken
- Whole grain bread for toast and sandwich
- Rice for stir-fry
- Pasta
- Chicken broth for soup
- Vegetable broth for soup
- Garlic powder for cooking
- Chocolate chips for cookies
- Black beans for quesadillas
- Corn for quesadillas
- Dijon mustard for tilapia

CONDIMENTS & SAUCES
- Marinara sauce for meatballs and cod
- Teriyaki sauce for tofu and mahi mahi
- Soy sauce for stir-fry
- Sriracha sauce for tuna cakes
- Pesto sauce for meatballs
- Pasta sauce for spaghetti squash
- Tzatziki sauce for snack
- Lemon butter sauce for shrimp
- Honey mustard sauce for chicken

MISCELLANEOUS
- Skewers for grilling
- Dates for energy balls
- Coconut milk for popsicles
- Almonds for energy balls

MEASUREMENT CONVERSION CHART

VOLUME CONVERSIONS 1

1 cup = 16 tablespoons
1 cup = 8 fluid ounces
1 tablespoon = 3 teaspoons
1 fluid ounce = 2 tablespoons

WEIGHT CONVERSIONS

1 ounce (oz) = 28.35 grams (g)
1 pound (lb) = 16 ounces
1 kilogram (kg) = 2.2 pounds

OVEN TEMPERATURE CONVERSIONS

Moderate oven: 350°F = 180°C
Moderate to Hot oven: 375°F = 190°C
Hot oven: 400°F = 200°C
Very Hot oven: 425°F = 220°C

COMMON METRIC CONVERSIONS

1 milliliter (mL) = 1 cubic centimeter (cm³)
1 liter (L) = 1,000 milliliters
1 gram (g) = 1 cubic centimeter (cm³) of water at 4°C
1 kilogram (kg) = 1,000 grams

COMMON INGREDIENT EQUIVALENTS

1 stick of butter = 1/2 cup = 8 tablespoons
1 cup of flour = 120 grams
1 cup of sugar = 200 grams
1 cup of brown sugar (packed) = 220 grams

VOLUME CONVERSIONS 2

1 tablespoon (tbsp) = 15 milliliters (ml) = 1/16 cup
1/4 cup = 60 milliliters (ml) = 4 tablespoons (tbsp)
1 cup = 240 milliliters (ml) = 16 tablespoons (tbsp)

BLOOD PRESSURE MONITORING LIST

DATE	SYSTOLIC	DIASTOLIC	MEDS TAKEN	WELL BEING / NOTES

DATE	SYSTOLIC	DIASTOLIC	MEDS TAKEN	WELL BEING / NOTES

DATE	SYSTOLIC	DIASTOLIC	MEDS TAKEN	WELL BEING / NOTES

DATE	SYSTOLIC	DIASTOLIC	MEDS TAKEN	WELL BEING / NOTES